ABOUT THE

J.A. Link has been a practicing ......gist, technologist, programme manager and service and enterprise architecture consultant since the 1990's working with a wide and diverse range of SMEs, global organisations and public sector clients.

For information about Acerit Limited or to contact the Author, send an e-mail to ITStrategy@acerit.com

The I.T. Little Black Book (ISBN 978-1906510-060)

Designing the Future:

How to Develop & Implement Your IT Strategy

J.A. Link

*iSee*PocketAdvisor®
Making Knowledge Accessible

Matador
9 De Montfort Mews
Leicester LE1 7FW, UK
Tel: (+44) 116 255 9311 / 9312
Email: books@troubador.co.uk
Web: www.troubador.co.uk/matador

ISBN 978-1906510 527

*iSee*PocketAdvisor® is a registered Trade Mark of Acerit Limited.

Mixed Sources
Product group from well-managed
forests and other controlled sources
www.fsc.org Cert no. TT-COC-2082
© 1996 Forest Stewardship Council

Typeset in 10pt Gill by Troubador Publishing Ltd, Leicester, UK
Printed in the UK by The Cromwell Press Ltd, Trowbridge, Wilts, UK

Matador is an imprint of Troubador Publishing Ltd

We can be heroes just for one day

About this book

Think it might be a good idea to develop an IT strategy but don't know where to start?

Had developing your organisation's IT strategy added to your annual objectives and need some help?

The fact you're reading this *iSee*PocketAdvisor® means you fall under one of the above, a variation of the above, wish to develop your current knowledge and confidence quickly or, are simply curious.

Whatever your reason for reading, rest assured our reason for creating this *iSee*PocketAdvisor® was to demystify strategy as a concept and as an activity.

Mainly due to intimidating, and often conflicting, academic research and weighty volumes written by 'grey beards', too many people remain put off, or afraid, to even attempt to develop an IT strategy.

Where to begin? What should it look like? What if I get it wrong? These are too frequently the initial questions and anxieties associated with developing any type of strategy. Consequently, this book aims to walk you through some of the considerations and key techniques – in plain English!

For ease of use, the book is logically organised according to the IT strategy development process; Plan, Do, Transform, Review:

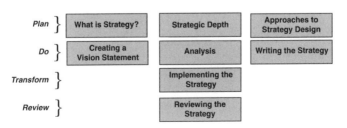

Each chapter begins by introducing some of the wider issues and considerations in developing an IT strategy, and dotted throughout the chapters you'll find some easy to remember icons:

Draws your attention to key points.

Indicates humorous examples to aid memory and enhance understanding.

Highlights the scientific 'smoke and mirrors' information.

At the end of each main section or chapter, a "highlights" section briefly summarises key points and a checklist is provided to assist you to prioritise your activities. Case studies are included to practically illustrate what can go well and what can go wrong when developing and implementing your strategy.

The detail contained within the book is neither definitive nor prescriptive. It is of benefit to both the aspiring and established IT professional as well as the novice, i.e., those considering a career in IT, teachers and lecturers, students, business managers, recruiters, career advisors, coaches and mentors, business consultants and leaders.

All details contained within the book were accurate at the time of going to print.

I trust you will find this *iSeePocketAdvisor*® both informative and useful.

J.A. Link
MBA, Cert.Ed., MIoD.

Contents

Chapter 3: Transform

Chapter 4: Review

Appendices

Figures, Tables and Case Studies

Figures

Tables

Case Studies

Introduction

It is still usual today to find IT strategies designed without fully considering and aligning with the expanded range of corporate drivers. They frequently take a narrow view of IT's place in enabling the organisation to benefit and prosper. For example, such strategies often focus on technology refresh imperatives or industry recognised process implementation initiatives.

Though these strategies may be appropriate for the organisation's size, needs and objectives, they omit the potential benefits which may be gained from designing and implementing a fully business aligned, and layered, IT strategy i.e., analysing and taking into account all relevant drivers and specifically developing an IT strategy which addresses knowledge management, information management, business systems (software) development and, technology and services.

Therefore, this *iSeePocketAdvisor*® has been designed and written in accessible friendly language to speed up your understanding and confidence level. It may be used as an aid to education and training or as a handy trusted advisor for the practitioner – allowing you to quickly dip in and out of the content as required.

Chapter 1: *Plan* is specifically written to assist you in planning your IT strategy; the strategic depth and the approach you're going to take during development and implementation. The chapter therefore explains what strategy is and isn't, the reasons and key organisational drivers for developing a strategy and, the strategy development process. The four layers of an IT strategy are examined – knowledge, information, software systems and technology and service – and the various approaches to strategy design are discussed within the context of organisational culture. The key reasons for resistance to change have also be included to help you ensure your IT strategy's implementation programme, or project, has the best possible chance of success.

2: *Do* focuses on the production of the IT strategy vision statement, carrying out 'as is' analysis using a variety of tools and techniques and, the production of the written IT strategy document. A template IT strategy document is provided to which you may add, amend or delete sections.

Chapter 3: *Transform* begins with considering the essential leadership style of the IT strategy implementer; including personal qualities and leadership characteristics. Suggested industry recognised implementation frameworks are provided as are example terms of reference for a sponsoring group, project sponsor, programme/project manager, a business group and technical forum. Some approaches for creating a timescaled programme, or project plan are listed together with some considerations for risk management, change and stakeholder management. Because programmes and projects rarely go to plan, also included are the five main reasons for failure with some advice should any occur.

Chapter 4: *Review* outlines the benefits of IT governance and ensuring you regularly review your IT strategy – both during its creation and implementation. IT Steering Committee terms of reference are provided to assist you with initiating your own review team.

Some appendices containing further information and the more complicated detail – such as ROI appraisal – are attached, as is a glossary, the Internet addresses of some related organisations and, some space in which you may make your own notes.

It's advised that you read all the chapters prior to jumping in and getting started with your IT strategy. This will ensure you're fully aware, and have fully considered, all your options.

Finally, I sincerely wish you every success in designing, developing and implementing your IT strategy. I guarantee it won't be easy; but then all things are difficult before they become easy.

Chapter 1
Stage: Plan

"The best way to predict the future is to invent it."
Immanuel Kant

The aims of this chapter are to clarify what strategy is and isn't, explore the reasons for developing an IT strategy, present the IT strategy development process and, explore IT strategic depth. Strategic depth includes explanations of all four layers of an IT strategy – knowledge, information, software systems and technology and services.

Additionally, consideration of the various approaches to strategy design and development are presented to enable you to ensure your chosen approach closely matches organisational needs and expectations.

Highlight summaries and checklists are included at the end of each section to assist you.

It is advisable to read the whole chapter prior to planning your IT strategy.

What is strategy?

Primarily, remember that strategy doesn't have to be difficult to grasp. It doesn't have to boggle your mind and give you sweaty palms. Equally, you don't need to hold a Master of Business Administration Degree to be able to develop an IT strategy; despite the generally accepted view put forward by some consultancies who like to baffle you with buzzwords.

No IT strategy can be scientifically proven to work in advance of implementation − it can't be *guaranteed* to reap the originally desired benefits. Indeed, let me share the most guarded secret concerning IT strategy with you:

! ● The Secret: There are no *right* and no *wrong* IT strategies − only those that succeeded in remaining aligned to business aims and objectives through regular review - and those that fail to do so.

Think about it. You may often read about over budget and over due IT projects, but when was the last time you read about an unsuccessful IT strategy? Yet, there are many articles in both industry and academic journals informing us of so-and-so's ground-breaking strategy. It's a simple fact that truly great IT strategies are only great with the benefit of hindsight − when they've achieved something. I say 'something', as quite often; strategies don't always achieve their originally intended outcome. They can sometimes achieve something totally unforeseen, or something not originally desired yet beneficial.

Strategies and strategic documents outline the general future steps one intends to take – usually over no more than a 2-3 year period. Lacking a crystal ball and the benefit of foresight they are, by their very nature, *best guesses*. They are an attempt to manage future uncertainty to the benefit of the organisation and provide a high level outline of the key steps to be taken in response to business need(s) or requirement(s). All IT strategies therefore need to be business aligned and, underpinned with business requirements.

To manage uncertainty we develop our own everyday strategies – making sure we're wearing clean underwear just in case we're knocked down and taken to hospital.

Strategies communicate where the organisation's going and, in a general sense, how the organisation's going to get there.

In simple terms, a strategy is the long-range, general direction you intend to follow to achieve a particular thing. For example, a personal strategy to live in a bigger house might include the general steps of gaining additional qualifications to enable you to apply for a better paid job which, in turn, will allow you to buy a bigger house.

Using this example, your end 'vision' is to live in a bigger house. Your strategy in achieving this vision includes gaining additional qualifications and then, using these qualifications, applying for and obtaining a better paid job.

All strategies contain the same elements as this example i.e., a vision and the general steps, or direction, to be taken in achieving the vision.

It's as simple as that. Unless you'd prefer some smoke and mirrors:

Strategy: Typically an idea that distinguishes a course of action by its hypothesis that a certain future position offers an advantage.

What a strategy isn't

It isn't a tactical, detailed operational plan written in techno jargon to deliberately confuse the Chief Executive Officer (CEO). Why should the CEO understand an internal class B IP address network topology with DHCP on your 100 Base-T LAN? Let's say their background is finance, do you think they'd expect you to understand the nuances of the accruals principle?

It's not about writing 100+ pages of poorly thought out random ideas in the hope everyone will be impressed with the thickness of the document; a case of, "never mind the quality feel the width!"

Good IT strategies are not judged by the number of pages but by the degree of business alignment and quality of thought.

It's not meant to mirror your own ambitions but rather, the ambitions (read goals, aims and objectives) of the organisation.

Strategies are not meant to be kept a secret, locked in a drawer and forgotten about. They're *living* documents meant to be communicated, regularly reviewed and refined.

"Communication leads to community, that is, to understanding, intimacy and mutual valuing." (Rollo May, American existential psychologist, 1909-1994)

CASE STUDY: Hope Inc.

A board level Chief Information Officer (CIO) was asked to outline their IT strategy by colleagues during a board meeting. The CIO became very defensive and turned to the Marketing Director saying, "Where's your strategy? Show me your strategy and I'll share mine with you."

The CIO was replaced within 6 months.

Had the CIO enquired as to why their colleagues were asking about the IT strategy they would have discovered the Managing Directors' concerns. These concerns centred on the rising disenfranchisement within the IT Department, the spiralling costs of the IT technological infrastructure and the frequent business system outages. Most of the IT Department didn't know what they were supposed to be achieving and had little information regarding the organisations key aims and objectives. This in turn created very low morale which was beginning to seep through to other Departments – Departments directly affected by the frequent system outages the CIO's 'secret' IT strategy were causing.

The fact the CIO **did** have a clear IT strategy and was making good progress counted for nothing. They'd failed to manage the organisations expectations by not fully communicating their IT strategy and the planned outages – and organisational benefits – this would bring.

The CIO was replaced by a more communicative CIO who essentially continued to implement their predecessors' IT strategy. By fully consulting with the organisation and making determined efforts to gather organisational needs and requirements to ensure alignment with the corporate strategy, they achieved spectacular success in terms of creating appreciative organisational recipients of the IT strategy's outcomes. They were also able to demonstrate, in the many and regular communications sent to all staff, the valuable contribution toward the corporate aims and objectives the IT Department had achieved.

Why develop an IT strategy?

As outlined in the Hope Inc. case study, an IT strategy provides the IT team with some targets to aim for and, a sense of knowing where they're going – direction. An IT strategy also provides senior executives with confidence that the IT systems and services provided are developed, deployed and managed in a robust manner and, remain in line with organisational aims and objectives. Additionally, a published and well communicated strategy helps to manage business user expectations; those who will be directly affected during IT strategy implementation activities.

> An IT strategy provides the IT team, and the organisation, with a sense of direction.

Though the above are all excellent reasons for developing an IT strategy, the most important is alignment with the businesses aims and objectives. These represent the underlying reasons – or drivers – for developing an IT strategy. Unjustified good ideas are usually not enough on their own to convince organisational leaders to commit to, and invest in, a strategy.

Imagine you're one of the board of directors and your head of IT presents you with a strategy involving implementing a new software suite which will mean investing €x millions in the IT hardware environment to support it. You'd most probably think to yourself, what benefit to the business will this software bring? How will it improve the organisations profitability? Will it reduce our risks? Does it cut our operational costs in the long term? Will it improve customer satisfaction? How long will the organisation have to wait to achieve a return on investment? Who's going to support it? Can our existing IT suppliers support it and if so, will it cost the organisation more money?

If your head of IT hadn't considered any of these, or similar, questions you'd most probably be very unimpressed.

!
•

When developing an IT Strategy *always* identify the key drivers – the reasons – for its creation.

If you're given the task of creating an IT Strategy always attempt to find out the reasons for its necessity; find out the requestors expectations of the IT strategy. Are they thinking of a fully layered IT strategy encompassing knowledge and information management, business systems software and technology environment or...? When in doubt – ask!

Some strategies are driven by the need to reduce costs, some by the need to simplify or consolidate an over complex IT environment, some are designed to decommission unsupportable software, some provide the business and/or its customers with real-time information or to create efficiencies with ordering, order tracking and payment activities etc. Others are designed to transform manual processes into more efficient electronic ones and yet other IT strategies are designed and implemented in response to organisational growth, shrinkage, buy out or change of direction.

Figure 1 illustrates the key drivers and their inter-relationships with each other and the IT strategy.

Figure 1: Key Strategic Drivers and Inter-relationships with the IT Strategy

Ideally, the corporate strategy will have fully considered and addressed all the peripheral drivers e.g., profitability and relationship management, supplier requirements and expectations, risk management and legislative requirements etc. The IT strategy may then draw directly from the corporate strategy in helping to define its vision and high level aims.

It is often the case, however, that either no easily identifiable corporate strategy exists or, the corporate strategy that does exist doesn't fully take into account the full range of drivers. However, the absence of a corporate strategy is not a barrier to your IT strategy's development. Rather than having a document called "The Corporate Strategy", perhaps your organisation has a business plan, a list of high-level aims and/or objectives, a mission plan or a vision statement. Any of these will do. In rare cases where none of these exist due to organisational size, culture or lack of appetite for strategy as a concept, feel empowered with the thought that you have the opportunity to trail blaze – to position IT as the key enabler toward organisational success.

Lack of a formal corporate strategy document is not a valid reason for failing to developing an IT strategy. You can use business plans or the organisation's aims and objectives.

Equally, an existing corporate strategy may not directly address knowledge or information management as organisational aims or objectives other than detailing legislative requirements and, perhaps for example, the aim of lowering staff attrition rates to improve information and knowledge retention. And yet, the key strategic areas where IT is able to easily justify its existence in terms of enabling the organisation to become more efficient and effective are knowledge and information management – knowledge and information creation, identification, reuse, analysis etc.

In addition to the key strategic drivers for developing an IT strategy, some of the main benefits include:

• The creation of stakeholder consensus and buy-in. Stakeholders include your boss, their boss, your team, the general workforce, your peer group, your suppliers etc.

- Proactive management of stakeholder expectations, in terms of policy, costs, service deliverables, service continuity and availability, timescales etc.

- To enable performance improvements to be monitored and measured.

- To make best use of resources (human, financial, technological, processes, systems).

- To communicate intentions, as simply as possible, to the rest of the organisation.

To summarise, all IT strategies need to be designed and written within the context of the organisation to communicate, as simply as possible:

- What you intend to do.

- Why you're doing it – what you expect to achieve.

- When you intend to do it and for how long.

- How you intend to do it.

- Who will be affected.

- How you will measure your progress.

- How you'll ensure what you're doing remains valid i.e. business aligned.

 Strategies are all about future intentions – what, why, when, whom and how.

What is the most effective process for designing, developing and implementing an IT strategy?

The most efficient and effective high-level process to use in designing, developing and implementing your IT strategy is illustrated within Figure 2.

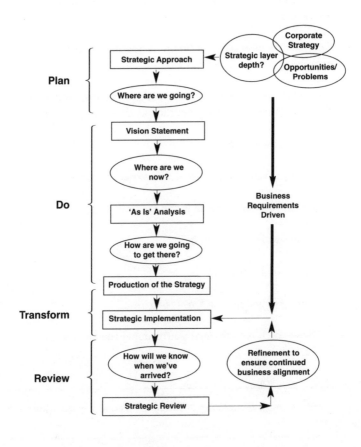

Figure 2: IT Strategy Design and Development Process

In Figure 2, notice the emboldened stages on the left - Plan, Do, Transform, Review - match the chapters within this book.

Tracing the process flow from top to bottom takes you from examining the corporate strategy and current business opportunities and/or problems, through to reviewing the IT strategy. At the heart of the process is ensuring the IT strategy is business requirements driven.

Defining 'where are we going' as the first stage of the process means no time is wasted in analysing areas of the current IT environment that will have little impact on the IT strategy produced.

Like using a road map; you need to know where you're going and then where you are now to be able to plan the best route.

Additionally, gathering the business needs and requirements early in the process – via, for example, the corporate strategy - assists with defining the IT strategy vision statement.

The vision statement provides many benefits throughout the entire strategy process. These benefits are contained within Chapter 2, Stage: Do, Creating a Vision Statement.

Familiarise yourself with Figure 2 so that you may more easily put into context each chapter's content as you read through the book.

Highlights

✓   There's no such thing as a right or wrong strategy; all strategies are 'best guesses'.

✓   All strategies contain the same key elements: A vision and the general high-level steps you intend to take to achieve the vision.

✓   Effective strategies are not measured in terms of the number of pages. It's business alignment and the quality of thinking that counts.

✓   The most effective IT strategies are those aligned to the corporate strategy – the organisations aims and objectives – taking into account the key strategic drivers.

✓   As strategies are meant to be communicated to stakeholders they are most effective when written simply – not in technical jargon.

✓   Lack of an organisational, or corporate, strategy is not a barrier to developing an IT strategy. Rather, it provides the opportunity to set your own boundaries in helping to enable organisational success.

✓   Following a logical and proven strategy design and development process ensures an efficient, comprehensive, aligned to the business, fit for purpose and regularly reviewed IT strategy is produced and implemented.

Strategic Depth: To layer or not to layer?

"IT strategy". What's included in it? What does the phrase conjure up in your mind?

Are you thinking of a document which details the future development, expansion or consolidation of your current critical business systems software?

Are you thinking of a document that will outline information storage, retention and retrieval standards?

Perhaps you're thinking of a document that aligns to some industry recommended framework? Or, maybe, a document that outlines how IT can further enable your organisation to create, effectively catalogue and share knowledge? Perhaps all of these and more?

In practice, the most effective IT strategies are those that encompass the following **four** layers:

- Knowledge

- Information

- Software Systems (Development and Integration)

- Technology & Service

A fully effective and organisationally enabling IT strategy comprises *four* layers – knowledge, information, software and technology.

However, in reality, whether your strategy addresses all four layers or just a few really depends on your personal remit as well as the size, type and complexity of your organisation.

For example, a small or micro sized organisation as outlined in Table 1 would probably view the creation of a full blown; four layer IT strategy as overkill. An exception to this would of course include the type of organisation where the core capability, products and services of the organisation centre on the creation and sharing of knowledge and information.

Table 1: 2008 European SME Definition Based on Headcount.

Enterprise Category	Headcount	Annual Turnover
Medium-sized	< 250	≤ € 43 million
Small	< 50	≤ € 10 million
Micro	< 10	≤ € 2 million

Note: In the United States of America the US Small Business Administration
is an independent agency of the federal government which specifies
small business size criteria (www.sba.gov/)

The A1 Printing Limited case study provides an example of an organisation where focussing only on the software systems and technology & service layers are appropriate. These layers were perceived to add most value to the organisation.

CASE STUDY: A1 Printing Limited

A1 Printing Limited is a 180 employee printing and packaging company with an IT team of 7.

The main business critical IT system – PrintIT – was used for production planning, estimating, costing etc. PrintIT was developed in house on a Unix platform; the system was secure and stable. Other technologies used included Apple for print and packaging design and Microsoft for email and web browsing. During the mid 1990's the web browsing and email systems were not considered business critical as customers could directly access PrintIT via ISDN links. This enabled customers to remotely view details regarding the progress of their orders, stock levels, account charges etc.

All customer data and information were logically stored on computer disk and no problems were encountered regarding sourcing customer data and information. A business intelligence software tool had been layered over the top of the PrintIT data and information; this enabled senior executives and account managers to interrogate the data stores and create customer ordering histories, future profiles, market segmentation information etc.

The 3 year IT strategy within the organisation focussed on the software system and technology layers. The strategy was designed and developed with the main objectives of:

- Further enhancing PrintIT's functionality – for both internal and external stakeholder benefit.

- Moving customer remote access away from ISDN and on to a secure web interface and,

- Lowering IT technology costs.

A good example of where a four layer approach is most effective would be an organisation with many and varied external Stakeholders; these stakeholders being both recipients and providers of knowledge and information.

A Stakeholder is any person or group with a close interest, or stake, in the organisation and its success. For example, members, employees, board of directors, shareholders, unions, general public, customers, suppliers etc.

In such an example, a top-down, requirements-driven approach to strategy development is most effective. Figure 3 illustrates the four layers in action.

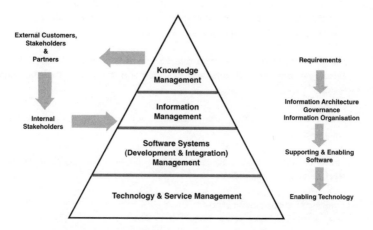

Figure 3: Top-down, Requirements Driven Approach to Strategic Design.

The gathered requirements from external and internal stakeholders shown within Figure 3 shape the knowledge strategy which in turn drives the information strategy and, informs the software systems and technology & service strategies.

This approach is also effective where the organisation's software development and operational IT infrastructure has been outsourced e.g., the Service Desk, Desktop and Server Management, Network Management etc. It's effective because the gathered knowledge and information requirements assist with the design of a service orientated Invitation to Tender (ITT) and Technical Specification documentation.

The benefits of a layered, top-down requirements-driven IT strategy are numerous:

* Enhanced knowledge creation and information sharing.

* Enhanced IT service delivery.

* Heightened customer perception and satisfaction levels.

* Stakeholder needs drive technology rather than the technology dictating or limiting stakeholder requirements.

* Improved supplier contracts and service level agreements.

* Robust IT governance.

* Strategically focussed growth of IT provision rather than organic, piecemeal approach. This, in turn, leads to reduced organisational costs.

So, which layer, or layers, are the most appropriate for your organisation?

One Head of IT didn't fully consider which layer or layers their IT strategy was going to address – consequently the vision statement definition process step took three months to complete!

What's the scope of your remit?

What are the drivers behind the need for an IT strategy?

To assist your decision, the remaining sections within this chapter provide more in-depth information regarding what constitutes a knowledge strategy, an information strategy, software systems strategy and technology & service strategy. By the end of this chapter you'll have a clear idea of the level(s) to which your IT strategy needs to go.

Highlights

✓ The most effective IT strategies comprise four layers – knowledge, information, software systems and technology & service.

✓ A top-down, business requirements driven approach to IT strategy design and development ensures continual business alignment.

✓ The decision to develop a four layer, requirements-driven IT strategy or to focus on only one, or some, of the layers depends entirely on your personal remit, organisation size, culture and corporate strategy (or business plan, aims, objectives).

Knowledge Strategy

A knowledge strategy defines the development of knowledge within the organisation and, when appropriate, can include the future development of sharing knowledge both inside and outside the organisation.

> An empowered organisation is one in which individuals have the knowledge, information, skill, desire, and opportunity to personally succeed in a way that leads to collective organisational success.

The purpose of a knowledge strategy is therefore to contribute towards the intellectual capital of the organisation – to the benefit of the organisation and, where appropriate, its external stakeholders.

'Intellectual capital' is knowledge that can be exploited for profit generation or other useful purpose. It includes the skills and knowledge that an organisation develops about how to make its goods or services; individual employees or groups of employees whose knowledge is deemed critical to a company's continued success; and its documentation about its processes, customers, research results, and other information that might have value for a competitor and is not common knowledge.

The beneficiaries of a knowledge strategy are most usually internal stakeholders; enabling them to work smarter and more efficiently, although many organisations such as charitable organisations also recognise the value of knowledge identification, creation, collation and sharing with external stakeholders.

But let's take a step back. What exactly is 'knowledge'?

It's knowing! It's the things we know. Knowledge is generally understood to be the body of research and experience of a particular subject or object.

Using the example of a book, data would be the individual words in the book, metadata the index (data that describes data), information would be the chapters and knowledge would be represented by the book in its entirety — the whole being greater than the sum of its parts.

To further muddy the waters regarding knowledge, it may be divided into two distinct areas — tacit and explicit.

Explicit knowledge is the knowledge that is written down, easily communicated, easily shared; otherwise known as 'common knowledge'.

 Explicit knowledge has been or may be articulated, codified, stored on media and readily transmitted to others e.g., documents, manuals, books, procedures. Tacit knowledge is much harder to access and share with others as, by its nature of being in peoples' minds, it represents ideas, thoughts and experiences. Accessing tacit knowledge usually requires personal contact and trust.

Tacit knowledge is held in people's minds and is difficult to access unless close personal contact and trust can be established. Most often it's tacit knowledge that's most valued by organisations — particularly the desire to tap into *customer latent needs* and specialist employee knowledge and skills.

 Customer latent needs are those needs customers are not consciously aware of.

Consequently, the most effective knowledge strategies seek to develop and exploit both tacit and explicit knowledge.

CASE STUDY: Bricks 2 Clicks Inc

Bricks 2 Clicks Inc. is a highly successful global, organisation which sells a wide range of goods solely via the Internet. Order fulfilment is outsourced as are secure customer payments. In essence, the company's core capabilities are service centric, i.e., Internet marketing and customer intelligence. This lean business model – and its proactive IT strategy - has allowed the organisation to become a hugely profitable business and enjoy levels of customer satisfaction and trust many similar organisations aspire to.

As the organisation began to gain success it realised it was transacting with their customers in a solely reactive manner - using customer previous purchase history (explicit) knowledge, and website statistics, to carry out predictive sales trend analysis and guess customer purchasing needs. This 'guessing' approach was proving to be unreliable as large quantities of stock were often unsold. The transactional relationship they had with their customers was one of supply and demand – they were in an asymmetric information relationship in that a transaction gap existed between Bricks 2 Clicks Inc. and their customers.

 Supply and demand concerns the economic theory of market value. Price is determined by the interaction of sellers and buyers to reach equilibrium prices which both are willing to accept.

Asymmetric information is where both parties to a transaction have different levels of information i.e., they are not symmetrical. For example, Bricks 2 Clicks Inc. did not *know* how much their potential customers were prepared to pay, what products they were interested in buying or, their latent needs.

Additionally, Internet frauds concerning website security for credit card payments were making news all over the world.

Bricks 2 Clicks Inc. quickly acknowledged that their reactive approach to identifying customer needs and customer security fears were the main barriers to sustained growth and, to overcome these would create competitive advantage for the organisation. They therefore redesigned and developed their IT strategy to successfully close the transaction gap; building customer service satisfaction, transactional trust and confidence levels whilst proactively identifying customer latent needs and enhanced tacit knowledge exchange within the organisation.

An example of a proactive knowledge strategy that develops and exploits tacit and explicit knowledge, both internally and externally with its customers, whilst proactively attempting to reduce asymmetrical information is illustrated within the transactional fold model (Figure 4).

Asymmetrical information occurs when one party to a transaction has much better information than the other. For example, a company's customers have a much better idea of what they desire than the company providing the products or services. Equally, current Internet buying habits are primarily held back by customer transaction trust concerns regarding credit card security etc. In short, this is creating a 'transaction gap' in relation to bringing the customer closer to the organisation. When the customer is brought closer to the organisation – by folding the transaction gap and reducing the asymmetries of information – the organisation is able to gather sufficient knowledge of the customer to provide efficient, customised services and products; as well as being able to more accurately identify customer latent needs.

The transactional fold model specifically aims to bring the customer closer to the organisation by closing the transaction gap. This creates continual learning for the organisation in terms of its knowledge about its customers. The model relies on IT and business alignment, robust underpinning processes, delivery mechanisms and quality assurance. Though, perhaps most importantly, the model requires innovative ways of identifying customer latent needs and, the provision of mass customisation opportunities. These may be realised by, for example, personalisation of the purchasing interaction and transaction activities, wish lists, previous customer recommendations and presentation of similar product options.

The vision and main objectives of the transactional fold model are to:

- Close the transaction gap between the organisation and the customer regarding customer needs; to create 'transactional fold' which:

- Enable the organisation to become proactive in identifying customer latent needs.

- Improve organisational customer intelligence (knowledge).

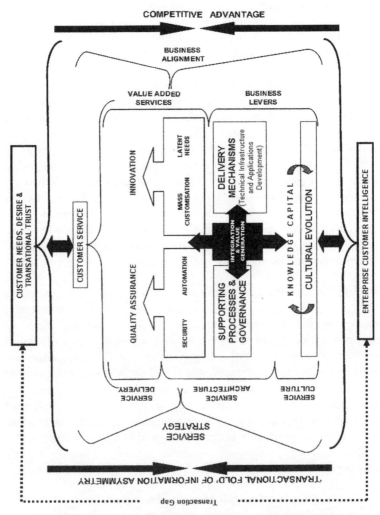

Figure 4: Closing the Transaction Gap - Transactional Fold Model.

• Continually build customer service satisfaction and transactional confidence and trust levels.

- Automate and exploit the organisation's existing systems and technologies.

In reality, most people struggle to differentiate between information and knowledge. Indeed the boundaries between the two are unclear primarily because an effective knowledge strategy relies heavily on robust information management. Equally, depending on perspective, one person's 'knowledge' may well be another's 'information'.

> Knowledge is what is known. Like the related concepts truth, belief and wisdom, there is no single definition of knowledge on which academics agree, but rather numerous theories and continued debate about the nature of knowledge.

The Knowledge Model at Figure 5, illustrates the strategic interdependencies between knowledge and information.

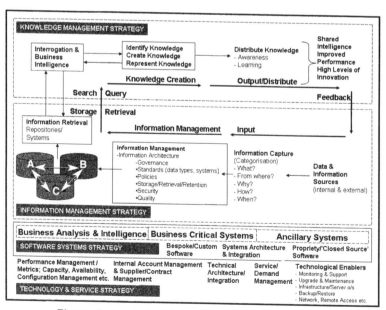

Figure 5: Knowledge Model : Strategic Interdependencies

As an aid to clarification; if your organisation manufactures widgets you may see limited value in creating a strategy focussed on the creation and sharing of knowledge whereas a research based organisation's core capabilities would include the development and sharing of knowledge. Equally, an IT call centre would see quantifiable improvements in both the efficiency and effectiveness of its operations where a knowledge strategy had been designed, developed and deployed.

 "It is characteristic of wisdom not to do desperate things." (Henry David Thoreau)

Examples of practical solutions designed to further generate and exploit knowledge creation and sharing include:

- Collaborative working applications (tacit and explicit knowledge).

- Email public folders (tacit and explicit knowledge).

- 'Lunch and Learn' sessions (tacit knowledge).

- Intranet forums (tacit and explicit knowledge).

- Research based IT teams, i.e., Futurologists whose jobs revolve around researching, communicating and exploiting new and emerging technologies (tacit and explicit knowledge).

- Implementation of concept models similar to the transactional fold model.

Highlights

✓ There is no globally accepted definition of 'knowledge'. One person's knowledge can be another's information.

✓ Not all organisations reap the same benefits of developing and implementing a knowledge strategy. The nature and culture of the organisation will often dictate the breadth and depth of a knowledge strategy and, therefore, limit or expand the benefits.

✓ A knowledge strategy concerns the creation, identification, collation and sharing of knowledge for organisational, and sometimes customer, benefit.

✓ The purpose of a knowledge strategy is to contribute towards the intellectual capital of the organisation – this may have solely an internal focus, external focus or both.

✓ Using the example of a book, **data** may be defined as the individual words in the book, **metadata** the index (data that describes data), **information** the chapters, and **knowledge** the book in its entirety.

✓ Explicit knowledge is knowledge that is written down, easily communicated and easily shared.

✓ Tacit knowledge is held in people's minds and is difficult to access unless close personal contact and trust can be established.

✓ Customer focussed knowledge strategies are most effective when ways are found to close the transaction gap; between the organisation and customer, by building customer service satisfaction and transactional confidence and trust levels.

Knowledge strategy checklist:

To help you decide whether or not your organisation is ready for a knowledge strategy, complete the checklist below. The checklist may also be used as the basis for developing a business case in relation to securing funding for resources to help you define, design and deploy your knowledge strategy.

Question:	Yes	No
Does your corporate strategy – or any business plans, aims and objectives – make reference to improved knowledge management; or similar?		
Does the size and complexity of your organisation necessitate a knowledge strategy?		
Do you share information and knowledge products and/or services with external stakeholders?		
Is 'knowledge' – its creation, collation and dissemination – a core capability of your organisation?		
Given the nature of your organisation, *should* knowledge development and management be a core capability?		
Is all information within your organisation (explicit knowledge) – i.e., procedure notes and works instructions – written down ?		
Would your organisation benefit from improved knowledge management activities?		
Does your organisation comprise very specialist job roles and functions?		
Is your organisation involved in 'cutting edge' research and development?		
Is it relatively simple and easy to source knowledge within your organisation?		
Do you believe your organisation makes best use of its information?		

Question:	Yes	No
Is staff turnover considered to be high within your organisation?		
Is working time regularly lost in trying to find and access information and knowledge?		
If the answer to the above question is "yes", could you estimate this time organisationally so that you can estimate the cost of non-productive time and rework?		
Within your organisation, is there a culture of knowledge sharing? For example, 'lunch and learn' sessions, staff bulletin, content managed intranet, staff forum(s) etc.?		

Information Strategy

An information strategy aims to define the future development, use and management of information within an organisation. It's about:

*   The type and nature of information (whether structured data held within databases or unstructured/inconsistently structured data held on, for example, email systems).

*   Where it's stored.

*   Storage naming conventions (file, folder).

*   How it's stored i.e., format and version control.

*   The security of the storage locations.

*   How and when it's retrieved and by whom.

*   How it's backed up, archived and restored.

*   The supporting processes, policies and people required to underpin the strategy.

 Information relates to specific events or situations that have been collated or received by communication, intelligence or news. Information is a collection of facts or data.

Additionally, legislative and international standards organisation (ISO) requirements need to be considered and incorporated where relevant, for example:

*   Sarbanes-Oxley (SOX) for public trading companies in the United States (US) including all wholly-owned subsidiaries and all publicly trading non-US companies doing business in the US. Additionally any private companies that are preparing

their initial public offering (IPO) will also need to comply with certain provisions of SOX.

• The Data Protection Act.

• The Freedom of Information Act.

• ISO 9001 (quality management system).

• ISO 27001 (information security management system).

• ISO 20000 (IT service management).

All organisations hold onto a wide range of information for a variety of reasons which include:

• Financial records (legislation and financial forecasting and management).

• Customer records and data (marketing, product development).

• Human Resource records and data (legislation, management, training and development etc.)

• Production and/or service records and data (forecasting and management, warranties, trending etc.)

Usually, the information is spread across different IT systems and structured databases; one for finance, one for production and production planning, one for Human Resources, various Microsoft Access databases and Excel spreadsheets etc.

Does the diversity of storage location create inefficiencies within your organisation? Do you know who is accessing what and when? Does data theft such as sales and customer information present a risk to your organisations business continuity?

These questions are important as not being able to answer them satisfactorily equates to a need for an information strategy.

> If you're not sure who's accessing what data and information, when and why then you probably need an information strategy.

For some very obvious reasons, including accessibility, organisations usually design their general information storage according to the organisational hierarchy. For example, a server 'shared' area is usually divided into departmental folders e.g.,

> S:\> Shared
> > Deliveries
> > Finance
> > Human Resources
> > IT
> > Manufacturing
> > Operations
> > Production
> > etc.

Within these top-level folders will be sub-folders for departmental teams. Within the structure each individual is meant to save their information within their teams shared folder – they often cannot save their information to any of the other folders as their access has been restricted for security reasons. Though this is an excellent reason for an organisational folder design, it also presents some limitations.

Unless a very minimal amount of the information held within the hierarchical folder design is needed by many departments to do their jobs efficiently and effectively, the design:

- Will create delays and bottlenecks regarding information flow and, most probably create an email burden due to requests for information.

- Create a situation where multiple copies of the same document are stored in various locations; hampering version control and requiring additional, and unnecessary, storage.

- Hamper new employees in terms of understanding the organisation and accessing required information quickly.

Imagine you join an organisation that has all the traditional departments such as Human Resources, Finance and IT etc. However, it also includes departments such as Standards, Policy, Governance, Committees and Statistics. You've joined the company as a Production Quality Manager and are looking to find out how to progress an application for additional capital expenditure. Where do you look? Policy? Governance? Human Resources? Get the picture?

"We can't solve problems using the same kind of thinking we used when we created them". (Albert Einstein).

It is for this reason that many forward thinking organisations now supplement the traditional departmental, shared server storage area with a shared area by output. For example:

        O:\>

                Accounting Policies
                Design Specifications
                Environmental Standards
                Facilities Templates
                Health and Safety Policies
                Health and Safety Standards
                Intranet Content_Historic
                Procedure Documents
                Etc.

In the above design all employees have access, and can save information, to all areas. It prevents storage duplication and eases the flow of information around the organisation whilst maintaining a 'confidential' shared folder structure for sensitive information.

Of course, the above design requires deciding on storage location, naming standard(s), retention, archiving and version control criteria – these forming the basis of the Information Architecture – a prerequisite, of any information strategy unless, of course, your information strategy stipulates the creation of an information architecture!

Information Architecture (IA) is defined by the Information Architecture Institute as (1) The structural design of shared information environments. (2) The art and science of organizing and labelling web sites, intranets, online communities and software to support usability and findability. (3) An emerging community of practice focused on bringing principles of design and architecture to the digital landscape.

In the context of information system design, information architecture refers to the analysis and design of the structured data stored by information systems, concentrating on entities, their attributes and their inter-relationships. It refers to the modelling of data for an individual database and to the corporate data models an enterprise uses to coordinate the definition of data in several (perhaps hundreds) of distinct databases. Additionally, at the higher level, IA refers to the definition of unstructured data stores (unstructured data).

It therefore follows that an Information Audit must first be carried out to be able to design and develop an information architecture i.e., discovering what data and information you have, where it's stored, current naming standards etc.

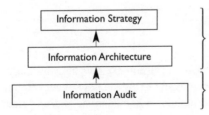

Figure 6: The Relationship Between the Information Strategy, Information Architecture and Information Audit

Finally, an information strategy needs to include reference to either the review or creation of information policies to ensure the continued integrity of your implemented information strategy. Information policy(s) need to include detail regarding email use, security, password length and complexity, internet browsing, data and information naming conventions and standards, version control, data and information re-use, physical and 'soft' security issues such as access to premises, confidentiality etc. For enforcement in maintaining information integrity and operational efficiency purposes, many organisations implement automated electronic document management systems (EDMS). Additionally, creating an organisationally dispersed team of data stewards or, centralised team of document management specialists, assists in ensuring information management remains robust.

 A large multi-national company engaged an IT EDMS reseller to implement their preferred system. The company budgeted £450K which included all consultancy and software installation and licensing. Alas, as the company had failed to carry out an information audit prior to engaging the reseller, actual costs soon reached over £1.2m!

CASE STUDY: Parcel People

As Parcel People's parent company was publicly listed on the US stock exchange, Parcel People in the UK had to ensure suitable and adequate management controls and governance were in place to meet Sarbanes-Oxley (SOX) requirements.

Parcel People's CIO became very concerned when the results of a SOX pre-audit indicated there were significant issues with the way in which Parcel People stored data and information. Security and confidentiality were inconsistent and ex-employee user accounts weren't being disabled. The CIO considered these inadequacies together with an internal IT process maturity assessment which reported that capacity management was poorly carried out and that data and information re-use opportunities weren't being capitalised on.

The CIO commissioned an information audit and using the results engaged a consultancy to assist the organisation in defining an information architecture. The CIO was advised that implementing the resultant information architecture would most probably involve considerable organisational change. Given these changes, setting up an information strategy would provide structure to the information audit, provide opportunities for the organisation to input into the architecture development and, provide a purpose – a vision - for the information architecture activities.

An information strategy project team was duly set up and the project initiated.

Although initially the organisation was reluctant to get involved with designing and developing an information architecture, it quickly became apparent to all that the benefits far outweighed the time commitments required.

The information strategy – with supporting information architecture – was implemented over a 2 year period. Benefits realised included:

- 40% re-use of data and information throughout the organisation.

- 35% productivity gains; i.e., less time spend looking for data and information.

- Significantly improved security and confidentiality; including security auditing.

Parcel People were successfully audited against SOX and ISO27001.

Highlights

✓ An information strategy aims to define the future development, use and management of information within an organisation. It encompasses legislative requirements, security (physical and digital access), storage, version control, use and re-use, naming conventions etc.

✓ Information may be structured (for example held in databases) or, unstructured (for example held within email systems).

✓ An Information Audit is necessary prior to designing an Information Architecture.

✓ An Information Architecture may be an input into the information strategy or, an output.

✓ Policies ensure the continued integrity of the implemented information strategy.

✓ Many organisations implement electronic document management systems to automate information management and related policies.

✓ Creating data stewards throughout an organisation assists with ensuring information integrity.

✓ A centralised team of document management specialists provides efficient and effective information management.

Information strategy checklist:

To help you decide whether or not your organisation is ready for an information strategy, complete the checklist below. The checklist may also be used as the basis for developing a business case in relation to securing funding for resources to help you define, design and deploy your information strategy.

Question:	Yes	No
Does the size of your organisation necessitate an information strategy?		
Do you regularly share information with external stakeholders?		
Is information – its creation, collation and dissemination – a core capability of your organisation?		
Is all information written down within your organisation (explicit) i.e., procedure notes and works instructions?		
Would your organisation benefit from improved information management activities?		
Does your organisation comprise very specialist job functions?		
Is your organisation involved in 'cutting edge' research and development?		
Do you believe your organisation makes best use of its data?		
Is your staff turnover considered to be high?		
Is working time regularly lost in trying to find and access information?		
If the answer to the above question is "yes", could you estimate this time organisationally so that you can estimate the cost of non-productive time and rework?		

Question:	Yes	No
Within your organisation, is there a culture of information sharing? For example, staff bulletin, content managed intranet, staff forum(s), staff briefings?		
Does your organisation have information policies regarding information storage, naming conventions, version control, access, security etc.?		
Do you, and your colleagues, know of all the information stores within your organisation – the structured (held in databases) and unstructured stores?		
Do you, and the organisation generally, understand the relationships between all the organisational information stores?		
Do your business users frequently experience difficulties in sourcing information; due to security restrictions etc?		
Is email becoming the main method by which colleagues share information within your organisation?		
If you answered "yes" to the above question, is email storage space growing rapidly making capacity planning difficult?		
Does your organisation already have an electronic document management system?		
Does your organisation already have a team of data stewards dispersed throughout your organisation or, a centralised document management team?		

Software Strategy

Software strategies focus on the overall future direction of the business critical and ancillary software held, used and identified as being of value to the business. Also included are consideration of software functionality enhancement, user interface improvements, integration, interoperability, consolidation, upgrade, management and the implementation of new business enabling solutions to address problems or identified opportunities.

Software includes all bespoke (developed in-house or by a software development provider) and 'off the shelf' commercially available software.

The majority of professional IT teams will hold information regarding all software used by the organisation – including server and desktop operating systems. If only to ensure compliance with licensing, this information is usually retained, and manually maintained, within a Microsoft Excel spreadsheet, Microsoft Access database, a configuration management database or, for example, a web based service catalogue.

Additionally, some organisations make use of 'seek and discover' software. This asset and license management software enables the organisation to automate its asset management; providing asset discovery, software usage and license compliance information.

 Many organisations develop software strategies to cope with regular upgrades to commercially available server and desktop operating systems; these strategies are more commonly known as 'technology refresh' projects.

Depending on the corporate strategy - business requirement(s) and need(s) – software strategies may encompass consideration of the improvement, implementation, decommissioning, insourcing or outsourcing of:

- Data warehousing.

- Data mining.

- Business intelligence.

- Integration and/or Interoperability with other organisational software and/or customer/stakeholder software.

- Embedding service orientated architecture (SOA) principles into software.

- Migrating user software interfaces into the organisations web browser.

- Creation or enhancement of web technologies and resources (Internet, Intranet, Extranet).

- Automated statistical analysis and reporting tools.

- Software to replace manual processes (internal and customer facing).

Data warehousing involves retaining all data (or a copy of all data) at one location; this location is then remotely accessed from any location.

Data mining relates to the automated search and filter of large volumes of data with the aim of extracting new information and previously unrecognised relationships.

Business intelligence (BI) is a business term used to refer to the applications and technologies used to gather, provide access to and analyse data and information about the organisation, its customer base etc.

Most often, the primary business drivers underpinning software strategies are to create efficiencies and reduce costs. It is always advisable to ensure the purpose, use, dependency and business criticality of each software package and suite is fully analysed and understood before devising a strategy which involves decommissioning.

Of course, any software strategy must also take into account resources other than the software. For example, where software is developed in-house, what impact will the strategy have on the existing development team? Will the team require additional training and development – at what cost? Will the strategy lead to a reduced development team and if so, how will job losses be handled – retraining, transfer or redundancy?

Where software development and/or provision is being outsourced, what will be the ongoing support and licensing costs? Are there any TUPE liabilities (Transfer of Undertakings Protection of Employment; UK legislation)? How will change management, software architecture, integration and deployment be handled?

What impact does the software strategy have on training and development costs and schedules, ongoing support and maintenance, contract management, business risks, health and safety, legislation, security and user experience?

CASE STUDY: Foil and Block Print Inc.

Foil and Block Print Inc. (F&BP) is a very large commercial printing business. In 2004 profitability was suffering primarily due to increasing competiition from Asia. The business analysed the market and their competitors products and services. F&BP decided that the only way they could successfully compete was on price. F&BP therefore began a restructuring programme and sought every opportunity to cut costs.

One of the high cost areas was IT and therefore the Head of IT was tasked with cutting costs.

After a review of the IT infrastructure, it was decided that significant costs savings could be achieved by defining a standard organisational desktop software image and removing the excess software.

One of the decommissioned software suites was costing F&BP £45K p.a. and was only used by one employee.

Unfortunately, it was only once the software had been hastily decommissioned and the employee's job made redundant that the organisation realised both the software and the employee were needed to progress orders through production!

Many orders were lost and the organisations credibility amongst its customer base plummetted whilst the software was reinstalled and the employee reemployed – at an additional cost of £24K p.a. ontop of their original salary.

Highlights

✓   Software strategies encompass all bespoke and commercially available software used within the organisation.

✓   Commercially available operating system software upgrades for infrastructure servers and user desktop computers are usually managed as a 'technology refresh' project.

✓   Though the reduction of costs is most usually the primary driver underpinning software strategies, careful analysis and consideration of each software package and suite must take place to ensure business continuity is not compromised.

✓   The impact of software strategies on other resources must be considered.   These include human resources, training and development, costs, support, contract management overheads, business risks, health and safety, legislation, security and user experience.

Software strategy checklist:

To help you decide whether or not your organisation is ready for software strategy, complete the checklist below. The checklist may also be used as the basis for developing a business case in relation to securing funding for resources to help you define, design and deploy your software strategy.

Question:	Yes	No
Does the size of your organisation necessitate a software strategy?		
Do you share information and knowledge with external stakeholders? For example, do you accept orders or payment via software solutions?		
Is information – its creation, collation, analysis and dissemination – a core capability of your organisation?		
Does the creation of management information reports take up a considerable amount of the working day or week?		
Would your organisation benefit from improved software systems interoperability with its suppliers and/or customers?		
Is your current legal position with regard to software licensing up to date and accurate?		
Is software asset management an automated activity within your organisation?		
Do your business users regularly request software enhancements and upgrades?		
Is working time regularly lost throughout the organisation in trying to operate your business critical systems?		
For any software application or suite, do your users complain that the manual system was much faster than the implemented software solution?		
Is it easy to share data and electronic information throughout your organisation?		

Question:	Yes	No
Do users of your business critical applications have to extract data and information out of them; import the data and information into spreadsheets – and similar – to enable full interrogation and analysis?		
Apart from password resets, do the majority of your Service Desk calls concern business critical application queries and incidents?		
Are all your software development projects and programmes carried out according to an industry recommended framework or method which includes quality assurance, governance, stakeholder appraisal and risk management; i.e., PRINCE2, PMI, MSP? (See Appendix 1)		
Does your current software provide the business with opportunities to maximise its effectiveness/profitability?		
Are your organisations senior executives confident that the business critical software provided is fit for purpose, efficient and provides value for money?		
Is your software secure and auditable?		
Is software systems architecture and integration an initial consideration of all your software development projects or programmes?		

Technology & Service Strategy

Technology and service strategies are designed and developed to underpin the knowledge, information and software strategies.

They concern the technological 'nuts and bolts' of IT delivery i.e., supplier contract and SLA management, relationship management with the business, hands-on support, security, technical architecture and integration, demand management, maintenance and upgrade of the server and desktop environment operating systems.

If you're already beginning to think the most appropriate and effective IT strategy for your organisation is going to be designed using all the previous three layers – knowledge, information and software systems - then this layer will be relatively simple to design and write as the requirements gathered during the knowledge strategy, and the outputs of the information audit and information architecture will clearly specify what is required by the business, how it's required, why it's required, the interdependencies, when and where.

 Refer back to Figure 5; Knowledge Model Strategic Dependencies and Figure 3; Top-down Requirements Driven Approach to Strategic Design

---

However, if your organisation lacks the appetite for strategy as a concept or activity or, simply decides it does not require a knowledge, information or systems strategy then the scope of your technology and service strategy will need to include all or some of the following:

- Business requirements for server services, desktop services, network services, remote access service, back up and restore service, change management services, disaster recovery services, information store(s) availability and access service, network service, business user support service (1st and 2nd line), security, integrity and confidentiality, project and programme implementation service, technical architecture and integration service, costs, timescales and performance metrics (customer facing SLAs).

47

- The future direction of the network (wide area network and local area network) – speed, capacity, availability, topology, costs, security, voice over IP use, monitoring and performance management, service continuity, disaster recovery.

- Remote access – security, policy, capacity, availability, costs.

- Data storage – configuration, location(s), capacity, availability, security, integrity, backup and restore, service continuity/disaster recovery.

- Server and desktop environment configuration, upgrade, lease, support, maintenance, hardware refresh, availability, capacity, service continuity, security, disaster recovery.

- Server and desktop environment operating system (o/s) type and configuration, location(s), licensing, security, upgrade, monitoring, maintenance, support, change management, service availability, capacity, service continuity and disaster recovery.

- Change management – for the back end infrastructure and customer facing services.

- Availability and capacity management – detailing how these elements are going to be dealt with.

- Disaster recovery – the strategy for recovering from a disaster, what constitutes a 'disaster', who may invoke a disaster situation and how the disaster recovery detail contained within the strategy aligns to the business continuity plan(s).

- Business user support - support hours, response times, fix times, categories of incidents, reporting metrics and user agreed SLAs.

- Project and programme implementation - available resources and the request mechanisms, costs.

- Technical architecture and technology integration - whether these are carried out, the need for these elements, costs, risks, alignment with the business and software development teams.

- Performance/customer SLAs – the reason for SLAs, with who they are/will be agreed, how they will be designed, reviewed, reported, reporting periods.

- Costs – infrastructure costs (hardware, software, telecommunications), human resources, training and development, consultancy.

Your technology and service strategy may frame all the above in terms of providing the strategic direction to:

- Outsource (or change supplier).

- Insource (bring all technology management back in-house).

- Partner.

- Improve customer satisfaction levels (internal and external).

- Improve security (physical and software access).

- Implement industry recognised practices and frameworks.

- Reduce licensing costs by changing the desktop and/or server operating systems.

- Implement data warehousing solutions.

- Implement storage area network (SAN) solutions and similar.

- Implement or decommission thin client technologies.

- Implement or decommission distributed system technologies.

- Improve service continuity.

- Improve disaster recovery arrangements.

- Reduce the costs of resources – hardware, software, people, suppliers etc.

- Upgrade/scale up the infrastructure.

- Reduce the infrastructure.

- Reconfigure the infrastructure (hardware, software, topology) in readiness for new business systems.

The list could go on and on in an equally daunting manner!

But, where do you start?

Perhaps due to the complexities involved with designing and developing a technology and services strategy, many organisations choose to develop strategies based on industry recognised practices and frameworks. These practices and frameworks are generally viewed as providing a structured way in which to *improve* the technology and services provided. When implemented in a comprehensive manner, and adapted to the nuances of the organisation, they provide consistent procedures and control mechanisms to the benefit of senior management, the entire organisation and, where relevant, external customers.

Industry recognised practices and frameworks include, for example:

- TOGAF® for enterprise architecture.

- MSP®, PMI® and PRINCE2® for programme and project management.

- M_o_R® for risk management.

- ITIL® and MOF® for service strategy design and service support and delivery.

- CoBIT® for providing an over-arching governance framework.

Figure 7 provides an overlay of the above for the typical IT department. It illustrates the areas in which the implemented frameworks can reap most benefit.

More information regarding industry recognised practices and frameworks are included within Appendix 1.

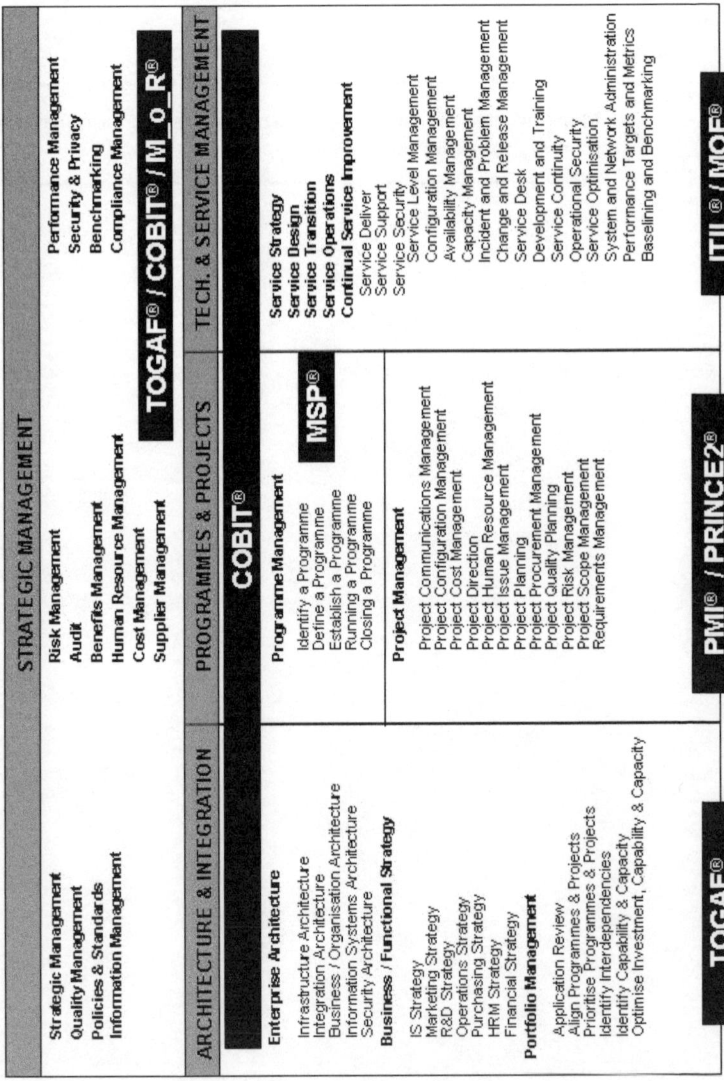

Figure 7: Industry Recognised Practices and Frameworks Overlay

STRATEGIC MANAGEMENT

Strategic Management
Quality Management
Policies & Standards
Information Management

Risk Management
Audit
Benefits Management
Human Resource Management
Cost Management
Supplier Management

Performance Management
Security & Privacy
Benchmarking
Compliance Management

TOGAF® / COBIT® / M_o_R®

TECH. & SERVICE MANAGEMENT

Service Strategy
Service Design
Service Transition
Service Operations
Continual Service Improvement
Service Deliver
Service Support
Service Security
Service Level Management
Configuration Management
Availability Management
Capacity Management
Incident and Problem Management
Change and Release Management
Service Desk
Development and Training
Service Continuity
Operational Security
Service Optimisation
System and Network Administration
Performance Targets and Metrics
Baselining and Benchmarking

ITIL® / MOF®

PROGRAMMES & PROJECTS

COBIT®

MSP®

Programme Management
Identify a Programme
Define a Programme
Establish a Programme
Running a Programme
Closing a Programme

Project Management
Project Communications Management
Project Configuration Management
Project Cost Management
Project Direction
Project Human Resource Management
Project Issue Management
Project Planning
Project Procurement Management
Project Quality Planning
Project Risk Management
Project Scope Management
Requirements Management

PMI® / PRINCE2®

ARCHITECTURE & INTEGRATION

Enterprise Architecture
Infrastructure Architecture
Integration Architecture
Business / Organisation Architecture
Information Systems Architecture
Security Architecture

Business / Functional Strategy
IS Strategy
Marketing Strategy
R&D Strategy
Operations Strategy
Purchasing Strategy
HRM Strategy
Financial Strategy

Portfolio Management
Application Review
Align Programmes & Projects
Prioritise Programmes & Projects
Identify Interdependencies
Identify Capability & Capacity
Optimise Investment, Capability & Capacity

TOGAF®

Highlights

✓   Technology & service strategies underpin knowledge, information and software strategies. Therefore, technology and service strategies are most effectively designed and developed following the creation of the knowledge, information and software strategies. This is because the knowledge, information and software strategies use a business requirements driven approach to their design and development.

✓   The absence of a knowledge, information and software strategy does not prevent the creation of the technology and service strategy. In such instances, business requirements must still be gathered to ensure business alignment.

✓   In the absence of any strategic ambition or vision to radically change the technology and service environment – for example, by outsourcing previously delivered in-house services – many organisations adopt and adapt industry recognised practices and frameworks to create efficiencies and improve customer services.

Technology strategy checklist:

To help you decide whether or not your organisation is ready for a technology strategy, complete the checklist below. The checklist may also be used as the basis for developing a business case in relation to securing funding for resources to help you define, design and deploy your technology strategy.

Question:	Yes	No
Does the size of your organisation necessitate a technology strategy – in addition to technology refresh projects?		
Is your organisation growing, downsizing or changing rapidly?		
Is internal customer perception of the services you provide average or better?		
In the event of a disaster, are you confident you/your team could quickly and effectively restore services?		
Do you suffer from frequent security breaches?		
Is your virus protection up to date and managed in a robust manner?		
Do you believe your organisation makes best use of its technology?		
Is staff turnover considered to be high?		
Is working time regularly lost due to corrupt data held on network resources?		
If the answer to the above question is "yes", could you estimate this time organisationally so that you can estimate the cost of non-productive time and rework?		
Does your user community experience regular, unexplained, service outages caused by technology?		
Do works instructions and procedure notes exist for all technically related activities with the department?		

Question:	Yes	No
Does your help desk/service desk run regular Pareto analysis/trend analysis (see Appendix 2) in an attempt to identify and manage down recurring support calls?		
Do you always carry out root cause analysis following major outage incidents?		
Does implementing hardware/software changes/upgrades/repairs frequently cause unexpected system/service outages?		
Do you have SLAs with all your customers for the services you provide?		
Do you provide performance information to your customers?		
Do you know how long it will be before your server/SAN infrastructure runs out of disk storage space?		
Do you know who manages all your supplier contracts?		
Are minutes of meetings with your suppliers taken and filed in a secure area?		
Are you aware of the cost of each service you provide to your customers?		
Are technology architecture principles applied each time the technology infrastructure changes?		
Do you have consistent and effective processes and procedures in place for handover from software development into the live environment?		
Is your license management robust and up to date?		
Do you know the cost of each support call to your help desk/service desk?		
Are your technical specialists regularly appraised?		
Are all members of your team encouraged to embark on developmental training (technical, process or other skills and knowledge)?		

Approaches to strategic design

The approach you take to designing and developing your IT strategy is critical and its importance should never be underestimated.

The approach concerns 'the way you do it'. This includes; what you do, with whom you do it, how you do it and when. In the long-term, ensuring your approach is aligned to the organisation's nature, culture and expectations saves time and improves your IT strategy's chances of success.

> Designing and developing your IT strategy without first deciding upon the most effective approach to take is like using your hand to try and push water up hill.

If the approach taken to design and develop your IT strategy isn't dictated to you by senior management, there are four main approaches to consider:

- Inclusive. For example, involving current departmental staff, peer groups, key suppliers, external stakeholders and senior executives.

- Inclusive with Consultancy. Using a mix of internal personnel and external consultants.

- Exclusive. Writing the strategy in isolation with minimal input from subordinates, peers or senior executives.

56

•   Exclusive, External. Using external consultancies.

Naturally, any combination of these approaches may be taken.

The approach you eventually decide to take will very much depend on the nature and culture within your organisation. The nature of an organisation includes its make-up, sector, features, history, life expectancy and ethics. Culture includes the experiences, attitudes, beliefs and values or the organisation.

Organisational culture is all about 'the way we do things around here.'

Let's run through the basic cultural considerations before moving onto examining each of the four main approaches.

Culture Considerations

Figure 8 illustrates the main purposes, dimensions, cultures and corresponding focuses and climates most commonly found within organisations.

CULTURE				FOCUS	CLIMATE
PURPOSE	PEOPLE / FLEXIBILITY	Personal	Individual	Person	Supportive
		Tribal	Team Team	Task	Innovative
		Matrix	Team Team Team	Output	Collaborative
		Collegiate	Collective	Co-operation	Consultative
	ORGANISATION / CONTROL	Fiefdom	Territories Territories	Competition	Competitive
		Command and Control	Hierarchical	Role	Conforming
		Rules based	Dictatorial	Power	Respect for Rules

Figure 8: Organisational Cultures

57

To assist you in more accurately identifying your organisation's culture use the following cultural characteristics table:

Table 2: Cultural Characteristics

		CULTURE	FOCUS	CLIMATE	CHARACTERISTICS
P U R P O S E	PEOPLE / FLEXIBILITY	Personal	Person	Supportive	Flexible working hours. Support available individually. Minimal supervision. Open communications. High commitment levels. Strong, shared values. Individual responsibility.
		Tribal	Task	Innovative	A diverse environment. Adaptive and change orientated. Focus on the individual. Flexible working. Solutions orientated. Proactive. Strong commitment; shared values. Strong/open communications.
		Matrix	Output	Collaborative	A diverse environment. Output/delivery focussed. Flexible reporting lines. Solutions orientated. Adaptive. Frequent organisational change. Responsive. Reward based. Policy and process driven.
		Collegiate	Co-operation	Consultative	Slow organisational change. Focus on the individual. Consensus orientated. Mediocre values. Varying levels of commitment. Open/high levels of communications. Plans. Policies.
	ORGANISATION / CONTROL	Fiefdom	Competition	Competitive	Similar dress. Highly competitive. High conflict. Diverse values. Strong commitment to differing objectives. Closed communications and information sharing. Strict timekeeping.
		Command and Control	Role	Conforming	Similar dress. Varying levels of commitment. Slow to change. Top-down communications. Limited career growth opportunities. Strict working hours. Productivity and efficiency based. Structured – centralised. Plans. Policies.
		Rules based	Power	Respect for Rules	Similar dress. Reward and punishment based. High levels of job insecurity. Lack of flexibility re: working hours. Owner-managed. Top-down, infrequent communications. Pressurised. Centralised.

Examples of a **personal culture** organisation include small Internet development companies and small charitable organisations. This type of culture would require you to ensure each individual is involved in the design and development of your IT strategy; that they're kept fully informed and, are given the opportunity to proactively contribute to its implementation.

Appetite for change is usually moderate and communications are most effective if delivered face-to-face. The speed with which you develop and implement your IT strategy needs to be moderate. If run using a programme or project management framework, the programme/project board membership should be selected from the organisation's senior management team.

Tribal organisations include software development organisations, media companies and event management companies. This type of culture would require you to take a very flexible approach.

Appetite for change is high though timekeeping may be an issue and therefore meetings would be best held in the late morning or early afternoon. Being an innovative organisation, you'd gain maximum value and support by firstly selling the benefits of developing an IT strategy, and then allocating tasks to teams by using a process of negotiation.

Communications are most effective if kept in writing, brief and regular, only focussing on progress related to task achievement. The speed with which you develop and implement your IT strategy needs to be moderate and you must be able to demonstrate some 'quick wins'. Again, if run under a programme or project management framework, the programme/ project board membership should be selected from the organisation's senior management team.

Matrix cultures are usually found within IT service supplier organisations, consultancies and where speed of delivery of products and services is paramount. Again, these cultures require you to take a very flexible approach – be prepared to adapt to changing circumstances. By being diverse and delivery focussed organisations, your approach needs to include regular and clear written communications regarding the strategic development process you're taking and, the envisaged deliverables (including timescales).

Appetite for change is usually only moderate – due to the necessary organisational changes which regularly take place a situation of change fatigue may well have been reached. In support of the collaborative culture, provide all those interested and concerned with the opportunity to input to the development process, the benefits, the vision statement and implementation.

The speed with which you develop and implement your IT strategy needs to be sympathetic to current work loads though it will maintain momentum if you deliver some 'quick wins'. If run under a programme or project management framework, the programme/project board membership should be selected from across the organisation's senior management.

Collegiate cultures most commonly exist within the not-for-profit sector, training organisations, consultancies, co-operatives, industry regulatory bodies and charities.

They are perhaps the most challenging to work within, as often, due to human nature, a polarity will exist with regard to working preferences. Roughly 50% will be go-getting achievers frustrated by the slow consultative climate; openly criticising the leadership team for their perceived indecisiveness, and roughly 50% will feel valued and listened to; expecting to be consulted on even the smallest matters.

Consequently, a range of communication channels and styles is best adopted. Face-to-face and regular written briefings focussed on all areas of the IT strategy need to be prepared and delivered. These cultures will expect to have their say with regard to every step of the IT strategy process and will expect you to listen and incorporate their feedback. Also be prepared for criticism yourself – you *really* can't please all the people all the time! When you become aware of criticism, deal with it immediately and in person. Listen carefully to the criticisms and try, wherever possible, to adapt your approach.

"We have two ears and one mouth so that we can listen twice as much as we speak." (Epictetus)

The speed with which you develop and implement your IT strategy needs to align to the culture's appetite for change and, usual consultative cycles – these are usually quite low and slow. If run under a programme or project management framework, the collegiate culture programme/project board membership should be selected from the organisation's senior management and key selected internal stakeholders.

Fiefdoms are most commonly found in higher educational establishments, utilities companies, some government departments and widely dispersed global companies. Senior management are often aware of the fiefdoms that exist, but view the conflict and lack of information sharing as a small price to pay for rising achievements, born from the competitive tension between the 'feudal lords'.

A fiefdom is a territory or sphere of activity that is controlled or dominated by a particular person (feudal lord) or group.

Within a culture of fiefdoms you'll need to understand the individual communication styles, work preferences, values and objectives to be able to adequately prepare your IT strategy approach.

Each fiefdom will comprise a diverse range of individuals and you'll need to gain their trust and respect very quickly. Talking in terms of organisational benefits will have little impact in terms of gaining co-operation and buy-in. You'll need to sell your IT strategy on an *individual* basis – 'how is your IT strategy going to benefit me?' – will be the first thoughts of those sufficiently concerned or interested in the IT strategy.

Appetite for change usually depends on the nature of the change, who is driving the change (i.e., to which fiefdom they usually belong) and, the degree to which individual fiefdoms are affected. If ran under a programme or project management framework, the fiefdom culture programme/project board necessitates senior executive membership from each fiefdom.

Examples of **command and control cultures** include local government, armed forces, health sector, construction companies, engineering companies, automotive and pharmaceutical companies. They are one of the most straight forward to work within.

Communications need to be top-down, clear and periodic. You'll need to gain senior management buy-in and visible support from the very beginnings of your IT strategy development. You'll be expected to work within existing policies and procedures unless you can demonstrate why these need to change.

Command and control cultures are one of the most straight forward to work within as long as you have senior management buy-in.

Expect to work with long serving employees who have extensive tacit knowledge of the organisation. You'll be expected to consult with those potentially affected by the IT strategy although you'll also be expected to demonstrate decisive leadership qualities. Everything must be documented and industry recognised frameworks are eagerly bought into.

These cultures usually operate a nine to five regime with flexitime for non-managerial staff so try to arrange important meetings either mid-morning or early afternoon.

Appetite for change is usually moderate although speed of change is usually slow. If run under a programme or project management framework, the command and control culture programme/project board must comprise only senior executives of the organisation.

These days, **rules based cultures** are usually only found in small owner-managed organisations such as marketing agencies, recruitment agencies, commercial sales and production organisations.

They are, in theory at least, the easiest culture in which to develop and implement an IT strategy. It's very much as case of - if the managing director has asked you to develop an IT strategy and you deliver one, or you deliver one and they buy into it, woe betide anyone who doesn't do as they are told!

Consequently, genuine appetite for change is difficult to assess although speed of change may range from moderate to fast. You need to keep communications brief and periodic so as not to waste either your time or anyone else's. Your approach needs to be clearly understood by senior management and they will expect regular updates with regard to progress, issues, risks and costs. Be prepared to have to change your strategy development process to accommodate changing business pressures, risks and opportunities and be prepared to change your IT strategy to accommodate a rising or falling budget.

Your IT strategy must demonstrate organisational benefit in at least two of the following: customer satisfaction, profitability, cost savings, reduced risk, and competitive advantage. If run under a programme or project management framework, the rules based culture programme/project does not usually required a 'board'. It is more usual for you to be responsible to the managing director, or one of their direct reports as your programme/project sponsor/director.

Now that we've covered the basics of cultural considerations, you'll hopefully be in a position to more accurately select the best approach.

Inclusive Approach

The inclusive approach allows for full buy-in throughout the organisation and strong communications from the start. It ensures everyone is informed of progress; supports a requirements driven approach to strategy design and development and, manages expectations throughout the development and implementation stages.

The most effective and practical way of using this approach is to create two distinct groups:

•   Business (User) Group.

•   Technical Forum.

The two groups are in addition to the IT strategy programme/project group who need to comprise an experienced programme/project manager(s) and architecture specialists as a minimum. The main driver, or programme/project manager, of the IT strategy usually chairs weekly or fortnightly meetings with the two separate groups; ensuring agendas are prepared and notes or minutes of the meetings are taken to ensure robust programme/project documentation is maintained.

It's usual to initiate and commence business group meetings prior to technical forum meetings. This prevents a situation occurring where the technical forum – the technology – drives the business. Once the business requirements have been satisfactorily identified, substantiated and included within the scope of the IT strategy, they are input to the technical forum for them to devise technical solutions.

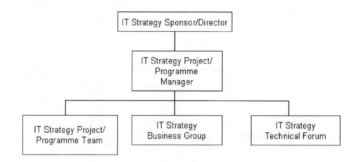

Figure 9: IT Strategy Design, Development and Implementation
Organisational Chart

The business group may comprise various levels of staff throughout the organisation – from senior executive to administration officer. Business system owners, key business stakeholders and representation from finance, IT procurement, and HR ensure the IT strategy develops in line with current business expectations, budget and policies and procedures. A maximum of 12 members of this group is advised – any larger or smaller and the group becomes too challenging to manage, or too small to ensure the full business perspective is considered.

The main benefits of using a business group include:

• Providing organisational assistance and advice with regard to business requirements.

• Acting as a communications channel, and co-ordination point for their respective departments.

• Provide support and ensure the business' expectations are managed and met.

• The subsequent IT strategy document and implementation activities will be 'owned' by the business from the very beginning. This reduces resistance to change and reduces risks.

- For continuity purposes, the IT steering committee (Chapter 4, Stage : Review) may subsequently be populated from members of the business group.

The main disadvantages of using a business group are:

- The number of members and diversity of the group usually means that it takes considerably more time to reach agreement. Members usually have conflicting ideas, expectations and levels of knowledge and experience with regard to developing and implementing an IT strategy; these conflicts and deficiencies take time to resolve.

- The group may use the meetings to score points against each other. This can include the IT department i.e., when business group members hi-jack the meetings to air their current dissatisfaction of IT services provided.

- Individuals may be unwilling or unable to 'see the big picture' i.e. members may put their departmental requirements first, to the detriment of the organisation as a whole.

The main risks of using a business group are:

- Individuals within a command and control hierarchical culture, rules based or competitive fiefdom may interpret any attempts to create an inclusive approach to strategic design as a sign of weakness – your and the executive management's weakness! Typically, this type of organisation expects "the boss" to be the strategist and present the strategy *they* have developed to *their* subordinates.

- An inclusive approach used within a collegiate culture may also produce a similar reaction, amongst roughly half the employees.

The technical forum needs to be composed of those individuals throughout your organisation that have excellent generalist IT knowledge and skills and, those with specific business critical IT system knowledge and skills; these individuals do not necessarily have to come from the IT department. If your organisation has outsourced considerable elements of the IT infrastructure (software development, systems integration, hardware support and administration) then it's advisable to involve your key supplier's technology specialists. Your suppliers will have the most current knowledge of your IT environment and, therefore, will be able to provide accurate advice and estimates concerning IT opportunities, costs, timescales and risks.

The main benefits of using a technical forum include:

•   The provision of a specific focus on technology; relieving the business group from having to fully understand all current and potential solutions at a granular level.

•   Motivates and involves – at the early stages of development - the individuals who will ultimately be responsible for delivering the solutions.

•   Acts as a moderator on behalf of the business. For example, a business requirement to transfer customer orders to call centre analysts telepathically would (for the time being) be rejected!

The main disadvantages of using a technical forum are:

•   The technical forum's ability is limited by its own experience and knowledge if technology specialists from key suppliers - or an experienced IT technical architect - are not included.

•   Technical forum members may also have a good view of the business requirements. This may mean they become members of both groups and, therefore, find themselves in a position of conflict regarding priorities and available time.

The main risks of using a technical forum:

•   In instances where the business group are failing to adequately develop business requirements, the technology forum may begin to take the lead. This undermines the whole process of developing a business requirements driven IT strategy.

* Business requirements outstrip the technical forum's ability and/or, the technical forum's ability outstrips the business group's ambitions or ability.

Inclusive with Consultancy Approach

The inclusive with consultancy approach is exactly the same as the inclusive approach but includes making use of external consultancy services.

It's not everyday that an organisation decides to develop its IT strategy. Consequently, the organisation may lack an experienced and confident individual able to carry the work through to business benefit. Consultancy services are, therefore, particularly useful in helping an organisation position itself ready for the project and actually get the IT strategy development and implementation activities off the ground i.e., setting up the process, managing stakeholders, risks and communications.

External consultancies engage experienced individuals who are able to rapidly add value to your activities. Particularly during instances of conflict and change, experienced consultants can ensure your project remains on track.

In organisations where the culture is tribal, matrix, collegiate, command and control and rules based, using external consultants particularly in the role of IT strategy programme/project manager adds most benefit.

Exclusive Approach

Using an exclusive approach to strategy design entails writing the strategy in isolation; with limited input from others. Of course, there will always be the need to ensure there's input from business users so that business requirements can be gathered. Additionally, technological and service groups and software development and integration groups will input 'as is' information.

It's usual to find an exclusive approach to IT strategy design taken within organisations with fiefdom, command and control and rules based cultures.

The advantages of the exclusive approach include:

- Speed. One or two individuals can develop and write and IT strategy much more quickly than a group or external consultants working alone.

- Focus. For reasons including organisational necessity, some IT strategies only relate to one strategic layer or one section of a strategic layer (see Figure 3, Top-down, Requirements Driven Approach to Strategic Design). This narrow scope therefore requires considerably less resources i.e., finance, human resources, information.

The risks associated with the exclusive approach include:

- It can prove extremely challenging to explain the detail of an IT strategy designed and written in isolation. This becomes evident when attempting to describe the strategy to, for example, a board of directors or line management whose specialist knowledge is not within the IT sector. Therefore time and money can be spent developing and writing an IT strategy only to then discover senior management's lack of support and buy-in.

- Selling the IT strategy to a wider audience is usually problematic. Within fiefdoms, where the competitive culture creates a higher than usual amount of resistance; disinterest, apathy and usurping activities may be evidenced. This usually continues throughout the strategy's' implementation activities and can result in only a fraction of the strategies envisaged benefits being realised.

Exclusive, External Approach

The exclusive, external approach involves using only external consultants to develop and write your IT strategy.

External consultancies can prove valuable as a support to developing your strategy i.e., interim resources acting as your IT strategy programme/ project manager, organising and running workshops, assisting with establishing the 'as is' situation by synthesising information and providing real-world experience in terms of what works and what doesn't.

However, no external consultancy can invest the emotional capital required to ensure your strategy fully aligns to your business – that remains your responsibility – it's *your* strategy *not* the consultancy's.

Remember! It's *your* IT strategy – not the consultancy's.

Additionally, once developed and written, who's going to implement the strategy? Either your staff will have to hit the ground running and potentially flounder or, you'll remain dependent on external consultants for perhaps longer than you had originally budgeted.

Usually one of the biggest mistakes organisations make, only realised with the benefit of hindsight, is to assume that using solely external consultants will save time i.e. because the organisation's team are working to full capacity and a strategy is urgently needed. It's a mistake because it is the organisations internal resources that have to provide the consultants with the information regarding culture, hierarchy, policies and procedures, business objectives, history etc. In the long-term, using a mix of internal and external resources reaps the most benefit for most organisational cultures.

Table 3 provides a mapping of organisational culture to approach. Using it as a guide, scrutinise the detail and decide which approach will provide the greatest probability of success for your IT strategy.

Table 3: Mapping : Culture - Approach

		CULTURE	FOCUS	CLIMATE	APPROACH
P U R P O S E	**PEOPLE / FLEXIBILITY**	Personal	Person	Supportive	Inclusive
		Tribal	Task	Innovative	Inclusive with Consultancy
		Matrix	Output	Collaborative	Inclusive with Consultancy
		Collegiate	Co-operation	Consultative	Inclusive with Consultancy
	ORGANISATION / CONTROL	Fiefdom	Competition	Competitive	Exclusive
		Command and Control	Role	Conforming	Exclusive / Exclusive, External
		Rules based	Power	Respect for Rules	Exclusive / Exclusive, External

Resistance to Change

Resistance to change is experienced no matter what type of culture dominates your organisation. Individuals are usually more concerned with themselves – self-preservation – than they are with the growth and improvement of the organisation.

! All organisations contain groups and groups contain individuals. The majority of individuals in our society are self-aligned (self-preservation) rather than organisationally-aligned. Unless an individual is driving or leading the change, or owns the organisation, their 'what's in it for me?' factor has to be perceived positively by them or the individual will most probably resist.

Put simply, resistance to change is human nature – it's normal.

When sagely 'grey beards' talk about maintaining the status quo, they're not referring to keeping everything exactly as it is. Status quo actually means 'maintaining the current rate of change'. Your IT strategy therefore presents a *sudden* change – a deliberately planned change rather than the slow encroaching changes the organisation usually experiences. It's therefore worth beginning to think about how you're going to manage resistance.

If a degree of resistance isn't experienced whilst you're designing and developing your IT strategy, then you'll certainly experience all or some of the symptoms when you begin to implement the strategy.

Symptoms include:

• Key stakeholder and/or group members failing to attend important meetings or always sending a substitute who's not empowered to make decisions.

• Arriving late for important meetings and arriving unprepared.

• Attacking or over-intellectualisation of initial ideas, scope of the IT strategy etc.

- Lack of positive input to workshop sessions, reviews etc.

- Building barriers – disguised as good reasons – to prevent progress – "we can't do that because…. (we've always done it this way / senior management won't like that / my team are too busy / we've got to do something else so haven't got the time to… /" etc.)

- Ignoring requests for feedback, information and/or not reading important emails.

 One organisation had so many resistant people claiming to have not received requests for information that the Head of IT had to put read receipts on every single email they sent out.

- Trying to attack you/your credibility by starting a whispering campaign behind closed doors.

- Making deliberate, audible and destructive remarks lacking justification, for example; "they'll never implement it", "it won't work" etc.

There are many reasons for resistance to change, these include:

- Fear of the unknown. Groups or individuals may perceive that the IT strategy will change the way they work to their personal disadvantage. They may also fear loss of power and control over tasks and, status issues i.e., how many people will report to them, where they'll sit in the pecking order.

- Jealousy – either of you or the IT strategy. Perhaps you're more personable. You may earn respect much better than they do. People may be jealous of your power; that they perceive you're 'liked' by the senior executives more that they are; that your project is bigger and more important than theirs. Jealousy is a very destructive and complex human emotion and there can be almost endless reasons for it.

- Anger. Against you or the IT strategy or even the idea of developing an IT strategy. Some people like having something to complain about; something to blame and, therefore, they're not keen to see a solution put in place.

- Insecurity. This includes both job insecurity and personal insecurity. Many people feel insecure in their jobs and you and your IT strategy may present a risk to their continuity within the organisation.

- Scepticism. Good old fashioned; "it'll never work / never happen".

- Lack of confidence and self belief. Some individuals and groups may privately consider they lack the skills, knowledge and capacity to learn new process, software, information storage policies etc.

- Misunderstanding. Some may misunderstand or misinterpret the IT strategy's vision, aims and objectives.

- Culture. This is relevant when the organisation has a history of resisting change; even throughout the senior executive team.

- Current work pressures and deadlines may genuinely create resistance with regard to taking on new working methods or training in new systems, processes and software etc.

- Disagreement. People who just don't agree with the IT strategy's vision, aims, objectives or the chosen solutions to be implemented.

- Change fatigue. Occurs when an organisation has already gone through numerous changes; individuals and groups are tired of change.

- Competitive 'turf war'. Closely related to the fear, jealousy and insecurity reasons for resistance to change, turf wars concern you and/or how the IT strategy may encroach into another individuals span of control, plans, ambitions and power.

So, what can you do to manage the situation? It really depends on your culture but in no particular order, you may wish to consider some of the following:

- Senior management support. Ensure the senior management team is united behind you. Without this you're chances of success are greatly reduced. This support has to be periodic and visible to the organisation – not just a 'nod' in a senior executive meeting. It's always advisable to ensure you have senior executive representation on your programme/project board or, as your programme/project director/sponsor.

- Stakeholder support. All stakeholders are not necessarily easy to identify. Stakeholders can be business critical system 'owners' or 'super-users', union representatives or highly influential individuals not necessarily high-up within the organisational hierarchy. You'll need to make regular contact with them to maintain their buy-in, keep them informed and calm any concerns they may have.

- Communication. Carefully consider how you're going to carry out communications and devise a strategy. This strategy needs to contain detail regarding; who you're going to be communicating with (list all stakeholders), the communication channels you're going to use (email, face-to-face, workshops, awareness sessions etc.), their frequency, style (length, presentation, key communication points) and tone (urgent, achievement based, informative, reassuring, friendly, professionally detached etc.).

- Education and training. All changes require a lesser or greater degree of education. Education and training includes workshops, awareness sessions, 'lunch and learn' sessions, presentations, floor-walking, on-line information provision, publishing frequently asked questions (FAQs), mentoring, coaching, internal and external courses. If your IT strategy is going to implement new software, processes or systems plan how you're going to support the organisation in adopting the changes.

- Support. Particularly when the reasons for resistance to change are fear, insecurity, lack of confidence and self belief, misunderstanding, current work pressures, and change fatigue. This may be on an individual level or organisational. Depending on the circumstances, support may be given individually, via presentations to groups, by positively acknowledging achievements and contributions, via reassurance, setting up feedback channels to encouraging two-way communications and providing education to those that need it.

- Build trust. Ensure you do what you say you will, when you said you'd do it and how you said you'd do it. If individuals confide in you their fears and anxieties etc., don't betray them. A good reputation is hard and time consuming to build – a bad reputation can be created in an instant; with one comment or action.

Table 4 presents a summary of the various reasons, symptoms and possible solutions to resistance to change. Study the table and begin to prepare.

Table 4: Summary: Reasons, Symptoms and Possible Solutions
for Resistance to Change

SYMPTOM	REASON	POTENTIAL SOLUTIONS
Key stakeholders failure to attend meetings; sending substitutes.	Scepticism. Misunderstanding. Work Pressures. Fear. Turf War.	Communication Build Trust
Arriving late for meetings; arriving unprepared.	Work Pressures. Misunderstanding. Scepticism. Jealousy.	Communication Build Trust
Attacking ideas. Over intellectualisation of ideas, purpose of the strategy, vision etc.	Turf War. Anger. Jealousy. Fear. Insecurity. Misunderstanding. Culture. Change Fatigue.	Education and training. Senior management support Communication
Lack of positive input to workshop sessions, reviews etc.	Lack of Confidence / Self-belief. Scepticism. Change Fatigue. Insecurity.	Education and training. Communication Support
Barrier building.	Turf War. Fear. Anger. Culture. Scepticism.	Senior management support Education and training Build Trust
Ignoring requests for information, feedback etc.	Misunderstanding. Scepticism. Fear. Insecurity. Work Pressure.	Stakeholder support Communication Build Trust
Attacking you/your credibility. Starting whispering campaigns.	Jealousy. Fear. Culture. Disagreement. Turf War.	Communication Senior management support.
Making deliberately destructive remarks without justification.	Insecurity. Disagreement. Misunderstanding. Change Fatigue. Jealousy. Fear. Anger.	Senior management support. Communication Education and training.

CASE STUDY: WF Motors

WF Motors is a global automotive parts manufacturer supplying the world's leading automotive manufacturers.

In 2001 the company decided to embark on an IT service improvement programme. The company sent key IT individuals on IT service management training with the aim of returning and cascading their knowledge and skills onto their colleagues. A project manager was appointed to lead the improvement programme.

One of the senior IT management group soon began to display many of the symptoms of resistance to change. Beginning with trying to destroy the credibility of the project manager, the resistant IT manager moved on to:

*   Openly critisising the project manager.
*   Questioning the need for the improvement programme.
*   Ignoring requests for information.
*   Failing to attend pre-arranged meetings.
*   Ignoring newly improved processes and procedures.

The project manager was puzzled by this behaviour and therefore queried colleagues as to what they thought could be the possible reasons. Many responded that the IT manager had long had issues with anger management and that he was the type of person that attacked and resisted change unless he'd thought of the project and, was implementing it.

The project manager made numerous failed attempts to get the IT manager on board. Eventually, the Head of IT raised concerns with the IT manager and indicated that his behaviour was not only jeopardising the project but was also jeopardising the IT manager's appraisal rating.

Though relationships between the IT manager and project manager remained poor, the project did complete to the benefit of WF Motors.

The IT manager subsequently left the organisation.

Highlights

✓ Your IT strategy development approach is all about the way you do it – what you do, with whom, how and when.

✓ There are four main approaches – inclusive, inclusive with consultancy, exclusive and exclusive, external.

✓ The approach you decide to take will depend on your organisation's nature and, particularly, its culture.

✓ Organisational cultures include personal, tribal, matrix, collegiate, fiefdom, command and control and rules based.

✓ The inclusive approach allows for full buy-in from the organisation and is most effectively implemented by setting up a business group and technical forum.

✓ The inclusive with external consultancy approach is the same as the inclusive approach but with the addition of using external consultants. External consultants used within this approach are able to guide, mentor and lead internal team toward fully realised benefits.

✓ The exclusive approach involves developing the IT strategy in isolation with minimal input from others.

✓ The exclusive, external approach leaves the development of your IT strategy to an external consultancy. Although initially considered to save time, considerable internal resources are required to provide the consultants with the data and information they require.

✓ There are varying symptoms and reasons for resistance to change. It's important to devise a plan for dealing with resistance during the IT strategy development and implementation stages.

Approach to strategy design checklist:

To help you decide on the best approach for your IT Strategy design, complete the checklist below.

Question:	Yes	No
Have you been directed to adopt a certain approach to developing your IT strategy?		
Have you established senior management's expectations of the IT strategy development process?		
Do you consider your organisations culture easy to identify?		
Do you believe you have the experience and knowledge to be able to develop and implement your IT strategy without external assistance?		
Are you able to create measures for dealing with any risks associated with your culture?		
Are you able to create measures for dealing with any risks associated with your approach?		
If appropriate, are you confident your suppliers will willingly contribute to your IT strategy's development?		
If you have already decided on your approach, have you established resources and a budget for its development?		
Can you identify your key stakeholders?		
Have you previously experienced or witnessed resistance to change within your organisation?		
Are you expecting a high degree of resistance to change?		
Have you made plans to deal with resistance to change?		

Chapter 2
Stage: Do

"I have been impressed with the urgency of doing. Knowing is not enough; we must apply. Being willing is not enough. We must do."

Leonardo Da Vinci

The aim of this chapter is to assist you with creating and writing your IT strategy; it includes creating the vision statement, gathering and carrying out analysis and writing the IT strategy document.

Highlight summaries and checklists are included at the end of each section.

Creating a Vision Statement

Plan }	What is Strategy?	Strategic Depth	Approaches to Strategy Design
Do }	Creating a Vision Statement	Analysis	Writing the Strategy
Transform }		Implementing the Strategy	
Review }		Reviewing the Strategy	

"Where are we going?"

Okay. So now you've got a good feel for what a strategy is, the layer or layers you're going to focus on and the approach you're going to take in relation to the design and development of the IT strategy.

Unless the IT strategy's vision statement has been provided by senior management, your next step is to gather business requirements. The gathered business requirements as well as the corporate strategy and business plan will help you, and any groups involved with the IT strategy's development, to create a vision statement.

 When developing an IT strategy vision statement, inputs include business requirements, the corporate strategy and business plans.

There are various ways to gather business requirements:

- Arranging a workshop(s) comprising senior management and/or key stakeholders; particularly those responsible for business critical systems and software. Prepare an agenda for the workshop to assist with identifying the requirements, for example, you could begin with identifying the business critical systems – their required availability, capacity needs, delivery (interface etc.), SLAs, etc. – and then carry out a SWOT (strengths, weaknesses, opportunities, threats) analysis.

Members of the workshop could write their SWOT for each system on post-it notes to facilitate discussion and enable them to be moved around.

• Prepare a business requirements spreadsheet and email it around to senior management and key stakeholders – remembering to provide a deadline for return of the completed spreadsheet.

• Analysing the current service provision, including all supporting 3rd party contracts, and comparing this to actual performance – where could improvements be made?

Once you have the business requirements you need to analyse them, for recurring or related themes and potential linkage to the corporate strategy. When this is complete, you can move onto creating a vision statement.

Analyse the business requirements to identify recurring themes e.g., improved service, business intelligence/management information etc.

Why create a vision statement?

Firstly, a vision statement will serve as a useful tool if your IT strategy begins to develop a 'wobbly wheel'. Wobbly wheels are those times during strategy design, development and implementation when the individuals or groups involved begin to steer the IT strategy, deliberately or inadvertently, off at a tangent. This may occur as a result of:

• Individuals or groups trying to take the IT strategy off in a direction that particularly benefits them rather than the organisation as a whole.

• Growing ambition for the IT strategy may begin to stretch its scope.

• Individuals or groups may seek to usurp your IT strategy; for

83

whatever reason they may deliberately seek to overcomplicate, disagree or attack the IT strategy process and your activities.

You can use the vision statement to draw these situations back; to remind groups and individuals of the shared vision.

Additionally, a short, simple vision statement helps to communicate the main aim of the IT strategy throughout the organisation and, raise awareness of the IT strategy's development.

 Short, plain English vision statements are the most effective way to communicate the IT strategy.

Ideally, a vision statement needs to be adequately informative yet vague – so as to allow maximum thought with regard to potential solutions.

Good examples of a vision statement would be:

> To consolidate our IT systems to provide improved efficiency and effectiveness.

> Improving our information management to the benefit of internal and external stakeholders.

> Evolving our IT services to enhance customer interaction opportunities and create internal efficiencies.

Vision statements are most useful when developed by a team, for example:

- Arrange a workshop(s) comprising senior management and/or key stakeholders, business group, technical forum etc. Prepare an agenda for the workshop to assist with creating the vision statement, for example, you could begin with identifying the recurring themes and/or relationships and dependencies between the business requirements. Use post-it notes for attendees to write down key words; arrange these to help to create the statement. If the business requirements lack ambition i.e., they all concern making things faster and more reliable, encourage discussion with regard to business ambition. Refer to the corporate strategy or plan to enable identification of relationships with the business requirements. You may also decide to invite your key supplier's business and technological specialists to this workshop – they may be able to add significant value with regard to emerging technologies and business practices.

If your vision statement workshop fails to produce a satisfactory, and shared, vision; this may be due to misunderstandings, lack of knowledge with regard to strategy development or, a lack of self-confidence on the part of your workshop attendees. Therefore, you may consider arranging some presentations to educate and inform the group. Examine your personal network for willing colleagues and ex-colleagues who would be prepared to visit your organisation and talk about what they're doing. Consider using your key suppliers or try to make contact with similar organisations to yours on the basis of a reciprocal arrangement – naturally, this wouldn't be an appropriate activity to pursue with your market competitors!

Once you've agreed a vision statement you'll need to expand it to set some high level aims, for example:

Vision Statement:
Improving our information management to the benefit of internal and external stakeholders.

Aims:
- To improve information management throughout (the organisation) so that internal and external stakeholders can more efficiently store, locate, identify, use and re-use data and information.

- Improve the access and presentation of internal business intelligence and management information.

- Improve information sharing throughout (the organisation).

- Improve information security and data access.

Once you've agreed the aims, negotiate and agree some targeted objectives, i.e., how you're going to measure your achievement against the vision statement.

Highlights

✓ To create your vision statement, gather and analyse the corporate strategy, business plans and note any upcoming opportunities and/or threats. Once this is complete, gather the business requirements.

✓ A good way of quickly gathering business requirements is to organise a workshop. Ideal attendees include; senior management, key stakeholders, supplier technological specialists, business critical system owners.

✓ Business requirements can also be gathered by preparing and sending out a business requirements spreadsheet.

✓ Create your vision statement within a workshop environment – this will help to create the 'shared vision' at the senior level. The attendees of a previous business requirements workshop would be a good choice for attendance at this workshop.

✓ A vision statement will help keep your IT strategy's development and implementation on track, helps to communicate the main aim of the IT strategy throughout the organisation and raises awareness of the IT strategy's development.

✓ The most effective vision statements are brief; not too specific and, written in plain English.

✓ Use the vision statement to develop high-level aims and objectives so that you may measure your achievement during IT strategy implementation.

Creating a vision statement checklist:

To assist you with creating the IT strategy Vision Statement, complete the checklist below. For each question you answer with "no", check to ensure you've given the question sufficient thought – that the activity or data and/or information regarding the question is not available to you or is genuinely not relevant/required.

Question:	Yes	No
Do you already possess the up-to-date business requirements?		
Has a vision statement already been provided by senior management?		
Does your culture support collaborative working in terms of holding and attending workshops?		
Is your organisation used to working to visions, aims and objectives?		
Do projects and programmes within your culture usually go off track? Or, suffer from 'scope creep'?		
Are you confident a workshop would produce a short, focussed vision statement?		

Analysis

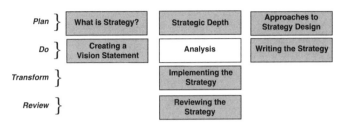

Plan	What is Strategy?	Strategic Depth	Approaches to Strategy Design
Do	Creating a Vision Statement	Analysis	Writing the Strategy
Transform		Implementing the Strategy	
Review		Reviewing the Strategy	

"Where are we now?"

Okay. Now that you've gathered the business requirements and created a shared vision statement, you know what the business needs are and where you're strategically going – i.e., what you're aiming for. You're therefore in a good position to carry out a gap analysis.

'Gap analysis' is a general term used to describe the difference between what is needed (business requirements and vision statement) and what is available (the current situation).

> A 'gap analysis' describes analytical activities designed to identify the difference between what is needed and what is currently available.

It's always important to analyse the current situation in order to:

* Help you develop your IT strategy. As you analyse the current situation – how you're currently doing things – opportunities, weaknesses, threats and strengths will appear. For example, you may collate and analyse your supplier support and maintenance contracts (who, what, why, when, costs, risks). This may reveal unnecessary complexity and/or lack of alignment to business requirements. You may also begin to wonder whether consolidation of the contracts would realise

significant cost savings.

- Give credibility to your IT strategy. It allows the audience of the IT strategy to put it into context. In other words, your analysis builds the case for the IT strategy – providing the reasons why the particular strategic stages are needed and, justifying their sequence.

 Plucking blue-sky 'good ideas' out of the air may be enough to convince you and your colleagues of the strategy's brilliance, but it won't necessarily convince the board of directors, who'll be looking for a return on any investments.

- Assess the 'gap' between what is needed and what is already available. This ensures you always make best use of the current assets – investments – of the organisation and, can provide a realistically achievable IT strategy in terms of complexity, timescales, degree of change, costs etc.

Therefore, your analysis always has focus. When beginning to carry out your analysis:

- Firstly, consider the business requirements – try to categorise these; for example, information management, service efficiency, business intelligence, collaborative working.

- Study the corporate strategy or business plans and align the business requirements to these wherever possible.

- What strategic layer or layers do you consider you'll have to go to in order to adequately address the requirements? Knowledge? Information? Software? Technology and Service?

- Find and request all information you think you'll need to analyse – try to obtain this in electronic format such as documents and spreadsheets. For example, server names, IP addresses, desktop assets, information storage locations, usage and spare capacity, installed server and desktop application, supplier contracts and associated SLAs.

* Put the data and information into some kind of order – related to 'where you're going' i.e. the vision statement.

* Use the analysis tools to either build a case for your IT strategy's direction and stages or to help you fully understand the current situation.

It goes without saying that the layer, or layers, to which your IT strategy intends to go will directly influence your analysis. For example, if your IT strategy mainly focuses on technology then analysis of the technological environment is appropriate. Similarly, if your IT strategy focuses on information management then analysis of the current processes, practices and methods of, for example, information use, identification, storage, re-use, naming conventions, costs, supplier support and maintenance would be appropriate.

 A technology manager given the remit of devising a technology and services strategy quickly enraged the Head of Business Systems by demanding a full written update of all development work in progress.

Analysis Tools

Analysis tools which can be used to help you assess the current situation and, assess the viability of potential solutions include:

General:

* SWOT Analysis. A strengths, weaknesses, opportunities and threats analysis can help to focus in on strategic prerequisites, priorities and opportunities. It can also help to identify risks within your current IT provision. A SWOT analysis is a good tool to use in workshops. Attendees can use post-it notes to write down their strengths, opportunities etc. The group can then discuss each and either move, agree or disagree with each

item. This is a good tool to use with business groups and technical forums to generate discussion and provoke thought.

- Pareto Analysis. Detail regarding how to carry out a Pareto analysis is contained within Appendix 2. Pareto analysis is more commonly known as the 80/20 rule. It helps to identify, for example, the category of IT support calls which creates the most issues. Knowing this information can provide justification for implementing service management and/or revising the organisations software development plans.

- User Panels/Interview(s). Similar to a workshop but including key business critical system owners and key users throughout the organisation. Setting up and running some user panels provides a quick way of gathering user perceptions of the services, software, reliability, availability etc.

User panels help to strengthen communications between the business and IT.

- Questionnaires (culture, priorities, service satisfaction). As long as any questionnaires are short, easy to infill and anonymous, most users are more than happy to complete one. Ideally, pilot your questionnaire with some colleagues to ensure it's kept as understandable and uncomplicated as possible. Think about the answers you will receive and how you're going to analyse them. For example, offering respondents the opportunity to write 'free text' answers is fine, but how are you going to reach conclusions from the results other than by trying to identify recurring themes? It's more efficient to provide questionnaire respondents with 'yes'/'no' options and sliding 'Likert' agreement or satisfaction scales – 1 (poor) to 4 (very good) – for the respondent to select one option.

- Workshops. Workshops should always have a timed agenda sent out prior to the session to ensure:

- All come prepared and,
- They achieve something rather than disintegrating into talking shops.

Ensure the people you invite to the workshops are relevant to the topic being discussed; small workshops of three to six people can produce similar results to an entire room full.

- Observation. Observe what's going on around you – learn to think with a critical eye. Are there regular visitors to the IT service desk due to a lack of call ticket acknowledgements? Observe the culture, attitudes and leadership styles.

Industry Recommended Frameworks:

- If your organisation has already begun to implement some industry recognised frameworks such as ITIL®, CoBIT®, MOF®, TOGAF® etc. Use a process maturity tool or consultancy to help you assess the maturity and, therefore, the continued development required to improve services, governance, enterprise architecture etc. One of the best known tools used is the CMMi®. CMMi® (capability maturity model integration) is an approach originally developed by the Carnegie Mellon University which is designed to guide process, integration and quality improvements. For more information visit www.sei.cmu.edu.

Financial Analysis:

- Particularly in instances where your IT strategy is going to be recommending investing in new software, technology infrastructure or process implementation projects, some financial analysis will be required. Remember, the IT strategy has to be agreed by the senior executives of the organisation and they'll require more than your recommendation to justify any increased expenditure. Two good methods for analysing financial investments are Return on Investment (ROI) and the Discounted Cash Flow (DCF) method. Details regarding what these methods are and how to carry them out is contained within Appendices 2 and 3. However, don't get too hung up with carrying out financial analysis particularly where your IT strategy concentrates on more intangible benefits, for example, improved customer satisfaction levels. Such improvements are very difficult to justify in purely financial terms – acknowledge and accept this.

CASE STUDY: ACME Bank

ACME Bank has branches all over the UK and totals 6,750 employees.

Whilst developing the IT strategy the CIO ordered the project team to send out a customer satisfaction questionnaire. The CIO preferred a 'command and control' style of management and, therefore, issued an email to the whole organisation informing that a customer satisfaction questionnaire was going to be sent to them and, that they had to complete and return it.

The project team put together a draft questionnaire and sent it to the CIO. The CIO tore the draft questionniare up in front of the project team and announced he'd devise one himself.

One week later the CIO emailed the questionnaire to the service desk and ordered it to be sent to all staff – this was duly done.

On the day of the questionniare closing date, the CIO approached the Service Desk Manager and asked for the completed questionnaires. The Service Desk manager handed the CIO a small pile of 50 (0.74%).

Although the questionniare received a poor response rate, the CIO decided to do their best in analysing the responses.

Unfortuantely, the CIO had not pilotted the questionniare – if he had done so, he would have been able to correct the spelling mistakes, typos and double-negative questions. The questions were also poorly ordered and many questions were designed to be responded to by inputting/writing free text comments. The comments input by respondents varied widely in terms of positivity and scope.

The CIO realised the questionniare had been a costly mistake. The poor design and small 0.74% response rate – an average response rate is 18-23% - meant that few conclusions could be drawn from the results. Additionally, the manner and tone in which the questionnaire had been distributed amongst all employees meant that a follow-up questionniare was out of the question.

Highlights

✓   The analysis stage is all about discovering 'where you are now', within the context of the IT strategy vision statement, by carrying out gap analyses.

✓   Analysis helps to develop your IT strategy, provides credibility and, helps to ensure best use is made of the current IT assets.

✓   Analysis tools assist with the gap analysis – general, industry recommended practices and frameworks and, financial.

Analysis checklist:

To assist you with your analysis, complete the checklist below. For each question you answer with "no" check to ensure you've given the question sufficient thought – that the data and/or information regarding the question is not available to you or is genuinely not relevant/required.

Question:	Yes	No
Do you have a good idea of the data and information you'll require to carry out your analysis?		
Bearing in mind your organisation's culture, would it be best to agree with stakeholders, a business group or technical forum the analysis you're going to carry out?		
Do you think your IT strategy will require some financial analysis?		
Is your organisation used to being presented with gap analysis results?		
Are any industry recognised practices or frameworks implemented within your organisation?		
Does your IT strategy have a vision statement?		
Are you clear about the strategic depth of your IT strategy?		
Can you obtain much of the raw data and information you require in electronic format?		

Writing the IT strategy

"How are we going to get there?"

It is usual for an IT strategy to have a three year horizon; implementation taking anything up to 18 months to two and a half years with the remaining time spent reaping the benefits i.e., realising the return on investment.

 IT strategies usually focus on a two to three year horizon. Any shorter and the strategy becomes a tactical plan; any longer and the strategy looses a sense of urgency.

The document you write will be the primary method of communication for the IT strategy. It therefore needs to be logically written for your audience and written in plain English wherever possible. Where not possible, use footnotes or endnotes and always include a glossary.

Much of the analysis you will have carried out will be complex. Therefore, use tables and charts to summarise the results within the main body of the IT strategy and contain the details within appendices. Make use of diagrams to simplify complex concepts and aid understanding.

The method of IT strategy development you've taken, e.g. business group, technical forum, etc., will dictate the approach you take to finalising the document. For example, if you've used groups during the design and development stages then it is advised to have the groups review each version of the IT strategy document before it goes to the IT strategy programme/project sponsor.

A generic outline for an IT strategy document is detailed below. Take out the sections not applicable to your IT strategy and include detail specific to your organisation.

IT Strategy Contents Template:

Title Page
Name of the strategy with time period (strategy title, 2008-2011), version number, organisation address and copyright i.e., Copyright (organisation)

Change Record
Date, author, version, comments.

Release Record
Date, author, version, comments.

Approvers Record
Version, name, position, date.

Keywords
For electronic information indexing purposes, e.g., "strategy", "knowledge strategy" etc. No more than half a dozen key words.

Executive Summary
Written last. Includes: very abbreviated version of the IT strategy, high level organizational benefits, relationship to the overall business strategy, resource summary including costs, summary of key projects and timescales.

Acknowledgements
Include all those involved with the development of the IT strategy, for example, the project sponsor, IT strategy project team, members of business groups, technical forum, key suppliers, key stakeholders and business critical system owners who have input data/information to the strategy.

Table of Contents

Tables and Figures
(summary tables and diagrams included within the IT strategy document to aid clarity)

Background
The organisation as a whole, and what developments IT has made recently. Include the reasons for the creation of the strategy.

Introduction
The purpose of the IT strategy, which layer – knowledge, information, software, technology and service – the strategy addresses, how the IT strategy aligns to the corporate strategy or business plans/opportunities/ problems.

Methodology
Strategic Scope (vision statement). Also include what's out of scope – say why the elements are out of scope for example, due to time constraints, internal prerequisites etc. Include management arrangements (your IT strategy project team – sponsor, project manager, business groups etc.).

Risk Identification and Management
Explain your approach to risk management. Explain how the main risks were managed (mitigated or otherwise).

Communications
Explain your approach to communications – the channels, frequency and audience.

Appetite for Change: Cultural Climate Assessment
Explain why you did this, e.g. so that the strategic implementation plans are aligned to the organisations capacity for change etc. Explain how you did this e.g., via email survey, workshop (if so who attended). Summarise the results.

Desk Research
List the documents you reviewed as part of your analysis stage, for

example, the corporate strategy, business plans, supplier contracts, maintenance contracts, etc. List any observations such as the condition of data and information held on shared areas (if appropriate). Include any recent organisation employee opinion survey results (EOS) if relevant.

Informal Interviews and Observations
Split interviews into two separate sections for internal and external. If you carried any out then explain them within this section. Say why you interviewed people, e.g. to raise awareness and gather business requirements etc. Regarding observations; you have attended some management meetings as the IT representative and been able to gather current business issues etc.

Strategy Document Review
Explain the review process for the draft(s) IT strategy document itself and also go on to explain the continuous review process, for example, via an IT Steering Committee comprising members from the business group/ technical forum or/an senior management.

IT Strategy Vision Statement
Duplicate the vision statement.

Aims

Objectives

Current Situation
Within the context of your IT strategy, outline the 'as is' situation; include elements such as resources, organisational design, suppliers (and costs), include any SWOT (strengths, weaknesses, opportunities, threats), ROI, DCF etc., analysis as summarised tables. Include diagrams to aid understanding e.g., network topology. An outline could be, for example:

Knowledge Management

Information Management

Software Development

Technology and Service Management

IT Resources (Team)

Contract Management

Customer Relationship Management

Management Reporting & Business Intelligence

Current Problems/Issues

Current Opportunities

Organisational Climate & Culture

Industry Recognised Practices and Frameworks

Governance

Costs

Business Requirements

Strategic Business Requirements

Relevant across the organisation and aligned to the corporate strategy/ business plan(s).

Business Service Requirements

Additional Business Requirements

IT Strategy 2008-2???

Introduction
Say what the strategy is designed to do and why.

IT Strategy Overview
Be brief in explaining the strategy in summary.

<u>The IT Strategy</u>
Explain the IT strategy in full. It is advisable to write this in a 'staged' or 'phased' manner. For example;

<u>Phase 1</u>: Implementation of Enhanced Document Management etc. (include all the detail for each phase or stage). Include any diagrams/concept models to aid understanding.

Envisaged Benefits

<u>General Organisational Benefits</u>

<u>Business Strategy Alignment</u>

<u>Efficiency and Effectiveness Gains</u>

<u>Knowledge Management</u>

<u>Information Management</u>

<u>Software Management</u>

<u>Technology and Service Management</u>

<u>IT Resources</u>

<u>Contract Management</u>

<u>Industry Recognised Practices and Frameworks</u>

<u>Customer Relationship Management</u>

<u>Management Reporting & Business Intelligence</u>

<u>Organisational Climate & Culture</u>

<u>User Satisfaction</u>

<u>Governance</u>

<u>Scalability and Future-proofing</u>

<u>Phase 1</u>: For example, Implementation of Enhanced Document Management.

<u>Outputs</u> (these are the actual deliverables of the Phase; they can be easily measured)

<u>Outcomes</u> (organisationally, for example; "it will be more efficient to retrieve information because...." These are usually more difficult to measure and, are applicable across the entire organisation).

Continue for each phase or stage.

Strategic Enablers

Explain what is needed to enable the IT strategy to be implemented. For example:

<u>IT Resources</u>

<u>Industry Recognised Practices and Frameworks</u>

<u>Costs</u>

<u>Culture</u>

<u>Organisational Values, Policies and Procedures</u>

<u>Governance and IT Strategy Review Cycle</u>

IT Strategy Implementation Constraints

Summarise anything that will constrain the implementation of the IT strategy, for example, a planned office move.

Implementation Roadmap

Use a diagram to show the phases/stages of the IT Strategy; include a time scale.

Glossary

Appendices

Highlights

✓ The IT Strategy document is a communications tool – always write it for your audience and in simple language wherever possible.

✓ Summarise your analysis findings using tables within the IT strategy document – attach the detail as appendices.

✓ Use diagrams to convey complex ideas and solutions.

✓ Consider the approvals process. Where you've made use of groups such as a business group or technical forum, ensure these groups approve each version prior to senior executive approval.

Writing the IT strategy checklist:

To assist you to write your IT Strategy, complete the checklist below. For each question you answer with "no" check to ensure you've given the question sufficient thought – that the data and/or information regarding the question is not available to you or is genuinely not relevant/required.

Question:	Yes	No
Did you use a business group or technical form as you developed your IT strategy?		
Are any key stakeholders expecting to be involved in the document version approval process?		
Do you have members of an IT strategy programme or project team who can proof-read the IT strategy document?		
Have you summarised all your analysis into easy to digest tables?		
Have you created diagrams to aid understanding with regard to complex current situations and solutions?		
Does your IT document *flow*?		
Are you confident anyone within the organisation could pick up your IT strategy document and understand it?		
Does your IT strategy document contain implementation phases and, are these timescaled?		
Are you confident you've carried out financial analysis on all aspects of the strategy which are appropriate?		

Chapter 3
Stage: Transform

"People underestimate their capacity for change. There is never a right time to do a difficult thing. A leader's job is to help people have vision of their potential."
John Porter

The aim of this chapter is to assist you to implement your IT strategy.

A highlight summary and checklist is included at the end of the section.

Implementing the IT strategy

Leadership Style

Before we begin to run through the various aspects of implementing an IT strategy, let's consider the important personal qualities and characteristics of your implementation programme/project manager. Remember, your IT strategy will involve transforming – changing – the current situation and, therefore, the project leader will need to possess certain personal qualities to ensure success.

Let's begin with first principles.

All success begins with self-belief.

Personal Qualities

Self-belief, without arrogance, is an important quality for the successful IT strategy implementer. Self-belief isn't about thinking you know everything – it's about having the confidence and trust in yourself to cope with the unexpected and the unfamiliar.

Self-belief usually comes to those who have regularly found, or put, themselves in situations beyond their experience and knowledge. They 'survived' the situation, reflected on it at some length and, learned much about themselves and others. The 'surviving' gives confidence and the 'reflection' provides heightened awareness.

Credibility is all about being believable and trustworthy. Believability stems from being qualified or technically experienced in some related task – possessing a specialism. Trustworthiness is earned on the job. People observe others all the time and make judgements based on their own perceptions. If you do what you say, deliver things when you said you would, support others and keep confidences, you will earn trust.

 Trusting behaviour and decisions are usually made up of an individual's perception of a cost/benefit analysis. Trust emanating from the 'cost' of trust not outweighing the benefits.

Charismatic inspiration concerns the ability to become a role model and in doing so inspire others to emulate you and achieve beyond their own self-perception. You therefore need to exhibit behaviours and attitudes that exude positive energy, focus, commitment, support, flexibility, humour, calmness and active listening. Any team is only as good as its leader, and the leader is only as good as their team. Poor leaders display many unprofessional qualities and behaviours such as; aggressive confrontations, backstabbing, derogatory gossiping and trying to destroy those they perceive as competition i.e., those better qualified, talented, experienced and professional.

 "The fish rots from the head" is an old Chinese saying which highlights the importance of the leader with regard to team success.

Optimism. Possessing the ability to pull victory from the jaws of defeat. Being solutions-orientated (task-orientated) with the ability to communicate both the solutions and an attitude of optimism.

Self-awareness. Understanding your own strengths and weaknesses and the impact your behaviours and attitudes have on others. Additionally, being people orientated with the ability to understand other people's fears, hopes and needs – addressing these in a non-patronising, flexible and supportive manner.

Commitment to the project. Determination, flexibility and persistence in the face of resistance.

The above is, of course, not an exhaustive list. However, it does represent the key personal qualities required of any IT strategy implementor no matter what the organisational sector and culture.

Leadership Characteristics

Hand in hand with an implementor's personal qualities, their personal characteristics are equally important. Characteristics may simply be defined as 'actions' and 'attitudes'. The key characteristics for success are:

Adaptability and Flexibility. It is rare for any project to run exactly to time, budget and anticipated outcome(s). Most often, this is due to resistance to change throughout the organisation, lack of resources, poor senior management support and/or unrealistic expectations. Consequently, the implementor needs to be flexible and able to adapt quickly to changing priorities and circumstances whilst maintaining their enthusiasm and optimism.

Respectful. The implementation project will create varying degrees of fear and uncertainty throughout the organisation. Symptoms of this uncertainty include; attack, jealousy, anger, insubordination, sarcasm, apathy etc. The implementor needs to maintain respect for all views and behaviours – understanding that these are not personal attacks – and listen carefully to all concerns. Throughout the history of the human race it is abundantly clear that being listened to is of paramount importance to the individual.

Rewarding. Every positive contribution, no matter how small, must be rewarded. Rewards include giving credit where it's due in communications, thanking people for their time and input and, in some circumstances, relating pay and bonus awards to achievement.

Organised and Consistent. A well organised implementation leader encourages all others within the implementation team to become well organised in turn. This creates confidence that everyone knows what they're doing. Equally, a consistent implementation leader ensures everyone knows where they stand, and how to deal with the leader. Consistent behaviour and attitude further supports the building of trust, commitment and credibility.

Select an Implementation Framework

There are many industry recognised frameworks you can use to give structure to your implementation project. Amongst the benefits of using industry recognised frameworks are:

- Professional, and accredited, training is available.

- Using a recognised framework provides a common language, and structure, for all those concerned with the implementation.

- Industry recognised frameworks are known to work effectively.

Appendix I provides information regarding:

- MSP® (Managing Successful Programmes); should you decide that the scope and complexity of your IT strategy is such that it requires a programme management approach to implementation.

- PMI® (Project Management Institute); a globally acknowledged project management framework.

- PRINCE2® (PRojects IN Controlled Environments) provides a robust project management framework.

Alternatively, your organisation may have developed its own programme and project management framework or methodology.

Ensure you're familiar and confident with using whatever programme or project management framework is chosen.

Establish Terms of Reference

Begin by setting up a project board and project sponsor – draft some terms of reference (TOR) for all the main roles. Ensure you obtain the approval of senior management.

Example: Project Board/Sponsoring Group (TOR)

The Programme Sponsoring Group comprises the Executive Management Team.

The Group will act as the reviewer and endorser of recommendations put forward by the Programme/Project Manager on behalf of the Business Group and Technical Forum. Additionally, the responsibilities of the Sponsoring Group include:

- Endorsing and supporting the Programme/Project Sponsor/ Director (PD); providing continued commitment and endorsement in support of the PD.

- Approving progress of the programme/project against objectives.

- Providing visible leadership and commitment to the programme/project at communication events.

- Confirming successful delivery and sign-off at the closure of the programme/project.

- Resolving emerging issues.

Example: Programme/Project Director or Sponsor (TOR)

The Programme/Project Director or Sponsor (PD) is a member of the

Sponsoring Group and, is ultimately accountable for the success of the programme/project. Additionally, the PD:

- Owns the vision for the programme/project and is its 'champion'.

- Secures investment required to set up and run the programme/project, and fund any transition activities so that the desired benefits can be realised.

- Ensures communications with key stakeholders are effective, managing the key strategic risks of the programme/project.

Example: Programme/Project Manager (TOR)

The Programme/Project Manager is responsible, on behalf of the PD, for successful delivery of the programme/project. Additionally:

- Facilitating the appointment of individuals to programme/project teams and groups.

- The effective leadership and co-ordination of the programme/project, the people and their interdependencies.

- Effectively managing all resources associated with the programme/project (teams, suppliers, costs).

- Working towards a position of consensus, with regard to the specifics of the IT strategy, amongst the Business Group, Technical Forum and Sponsoring Group; making justified recommendations to the Sponsoring Group for decision where consensus cannot be reached.

- Proactive management of programme/project risks and issues.

- Proactive monitoring and progress of the programme/project.

- Managing communications with Stakeholders; via established channels where appropriate.

- Coherence of the programme/project and development and maintenance of the programme/project environment.

- Drafting the IT strategy for Sponsoring Group review and endorsement.

Example: A Business Group (TOR)

Aim: To provide knowledge, insight and information relating to the IT strategy programme/project and, contribute to the direction of the IT strategy.

Whilst acting as a representative body of (organisation name) and, as part of the IT strategy programme/project, work with the Programme/Project Manager and any other related resources to:

- Provide, in a timely manner, accurate information and data which clearly defines the current 'as is' situation within (organisation name).

- Participate in any Stakeholder, Risk and general Gap Analysis workshops.

- Provide business critical information in relation to IT strategic development.

- Actively contribute to thinking, discussions and debates regarding the development of the IT strategy and future resourcing requirements; providing recommendations for review and endorsement by the sponsoring group.

- Participate in communication activities regarding the programme/project and act as 'champions' of the programme/project; providing visible support.

Example: A Technical Forum (TOR)

Aim: To provide technical knowledge, insight and information relating to the IT strategy programme/project and contribute to the direction of the IT strategy.

Whilst acting as a representative body of (organisation name) and, as part of the IT strategy programme/project, work with the Programme/Project Manager and any other related resources to:

• Provide, in a timely manner, accurate information and data which clearly defines the current 'as is' situation within (organisation name).

• Provide technical input, analysis and solution-orientated architecture (as opposed to purely service-orientated) options regarding the development of the IT strategy.

• Develop and evaluate proposed IT strategic direction for (as a minimum):

   • Degree of technical change required.

   • Business/Technical Benefits.

   • Stakeholder Benefits (internal, external).

   • Supportability/Maintainability.

   • IT Service Continuity/BCM.

   • Service Requirements.

   • Risks.

   • Costs.

• Actively contribute to thinking, discussions and debates regarding the development of the IT strategy and future resource requirements.

- Participate in communications activities regarding the programme/project and act as 'champions' of the programme/project; providing visible support.

Creating Timescaled Programme or Project Plans

Many people become very fearful of creating programme and project plans, either because they think they lack the skills and abilities associated with the planning software or because they simply don't know where to begin.

One of the most expedient ways of creating programme and project plans is to hold a planning workshop – a programme/project definition workshop. The aim of the workshop is to create a high-level programme or project plan.

Attendees need to be individuals with specialist knowledge of the area to be planned. If holding a programme/project planning workshop:

- Begin with referencing the vision statement, aims and objectives of the programme/project.

- Remind all present of the agreed programme/project stages as outlined within the IT strategy document.

- Do some 'brainstorming' using post-it notes.

- Discuss the results of the brainstorming to reach agreement with regard to the sequence and main activities, timescales and outputs for each stage.

Write up the results using project planning software and distribute this for review to all those in attendance at the workshop.

Once you have reached agreement amongst the workshop attendees, review the programme/project plan with the programme sponsor/director and sponsoring group.

Assess and Initiate Risk Management

Risk management is important because we do not live in a certain world and neither does your project! Therefore risk management seeks to identify, categorise, assess, prioritise and plan for potential risks.

Risks may be categorised in many different ways, for example, strategic, operational, programme/project. Equally, assessment of risks may include probability, impact, proximity etc.

Risk management makes risk(s) transparent.

Hopefully you will have thought about and prepared for risk management during the planning phase. Your organisation may have an established risk management methodology you can use to aid your programme or project. If not, one industry recognised risk management framework you may use is the Office of Government Commerce's (OGC's) M_o_R® (Management of Risk). Further information regarding M_o_R is contained within Appendix 1.

Once you've assessed the risks at the beginning of your IT strategy programme or project and documented them within a risk register, it is always a good idea to carryout regular reviews of the register with the programme/project team and sponsoring group/sponsoring director.

Set up Programme/Project Change Management

As you begin to implement the IT strategy, the implemented solution will begin to impact business as usual operations. Additionally, it is always good to have a programme/project change process in place so that team members, sponsoring group members and the sponsor etc. can request changes to the project. The change management process will provide a record of the changes requested, rejected and accepted.

A simple way of implementing a change management process is to create a "request for change" template. This template needs to include – as a minimum:

- A reference number so that you may easily reference each change.

- Date of the change request.

- The name of the person requesting the change, their telephone number, location etc.

- The nature of the change. (Explaining what the change is.)

- Justification for the change. (Why the change is necessary.)

- Costs of the change. Sometimes this can be completed by the change requestor, however, it is normally assessed by the project manager.

- Timescale for the change. Whether the change is urgent or, must be implemented at a particular time etc.

- Impact of the change. What the requestor envisages the impact of the change will be. It is common to provide categories for the requestor to tick e.g., programme, project, business as usual etc.

- Approval assessment criteria. This would indicate whether the project manager can approve the change (for minor changes) or whether the change needs to be assessed by a change board.

- Date of approval, rejection, on hold, returned for further information.

- Date of handover either to the project team or to business as usual operations for implementation.

Once the change template has been completed and sent to the IT strategy programme/project team, it is assessed by the programme/ project manager and may be rejected, accepted or referred to the programme/project change board.

The programme/project change board usually comprises members of the programme/project team, business group, technical forum, sponsoring group etc. The programme/project change board assesses the change request in terms of its scope, impact, costs and alignment to the programme/project.

If the board consider the change is out of scope, too costly, high risk etc., it will reject the change request and inform the requestor.

In instances where the programme/project needs to implement a change into business as usual operations, the programme/project manger will oversee the completion of the change template. This will then be directed to the business as usual operational change management process for assessment and release scheduling.

Assess and Initiate Stakeholder Management and Communications

It is unfortunate that sometimes a programme or project can be a huge success in terms of delivery but perceived by the organisation to be a failure. This is frequently due to poor communications and stakeholder management.

Stakeholder management is all about proactively managing stakeholder expectations, wants, needs and ambitions. Managing stakeholders reduces surprises, failure, risks and misunderstandings – it keeps the stakeholders 'on board'.

A Stakeholder is any person or group with a close interest, or stake, in the organisation and its success. For example, members, employees, board of directors, shareholders, unions, general public, customers, suppliers etc.

Think about who the programme or project stakeholders are. These will include the sponsoring group, project sponsor/director, unions, employees, suppliers, your boss, the managing director or chief information officer etc.

Use Table 5 as a guide to assist you in drawing up the stakeholder's interests and communication channels. You can then expand the table to include communication frequency. For example, you may meet with the project sponsor once a week and with the sponsoring group once per month or fortnight.

Table 5: Stakeholder Interests and Communication Channels

STAKEHOLDER	INTEREST	COMMUNICATION CHANNELS					
		Meetings	Intranet	Highlight Report	Staff Briefing (Verbal)	Staff Briefing (Written)	Lunch & Learn Sessions
Sponsoring Group	Budget, Progress, Outcomes	✓		✓			
Project Sponsor	Budget, Deliverables, Progress.	✓		✓			
Business Group	Outcomes, Deliverables, Timescales, Impact	✓	✓		✓	✓	
Technical Forum	Deliverables, timescales, solutions	✓	✓		✓	✓	
Business Critical System Owners	Degree of Change, Timescales, Impact		✓		✓	✓	✓
Service Recipients	Change, Progress, 'what's in it for me?'		✓		✓	✓	✓
All employees	Degree of change, when, to whom, how?		✓		✓	✓	

Managing the Project/Programme – Assessing Progress and Business Alignment

Once all the above has been set up and is working effectively, the project needs to be carefully managed and monitored to ensure continued progress.

A regular highlight report detailing progress against plans, the status of each workstream, issues and successes will keep the project sponsor/director and sponsoring group informed.

To their cost, an IT strategy implementation programme manager failed to highlight the successes of the programme along with the issues and delays. As a consequence, both the sponsoring group and sponsoring director mistakenly thought the programme was constantly veering from bad to absolutely disastrous!

Additionally, regular business group, technical forum and project team meetings will help to keep all those involved motivated, engaged and informed.

Keeping an issue register is a good way for a project leader to keep abreast of emerging problems. Set up a simple spreadsheet to document the issue, when it was identified, who identified it, who's affected by it, and what is to be done about it. A regular review of the issue register with the project sponsor/director and, where appropriate, the sponsoring group is recommended.

Don't forget to communicate project achievements to stakeholders; outlining the benefits each achievement will bring.

Continue to be resilient and determined to achieve programme/project achievements and closure against the vision statement.

CASE STUDY : Bodgeit & Dodgeit

Bodgeit & Dodgeit is a medium sized commercial organisation with all its IT provision (hardware and software) outsourced to one main IT Services Supplier under the terms of a 5 year contract. The IT Services Supplier provided a Service Desk function, problem management (desktop and server administration) and ad hoc projects costed separately, for example, technology refresh projects, server and related software upgrades etc.

Bodgeit & Dodgeit has a collegiate culture.

The contract was being carried out according to contract and SLA targets. The annual cost of the contract was c.£950K p.a. Internal business user satisfaction ratings of the services supplied were reasonable – most negative remarks concerning the IT Services Supplier stemmed from a lack of communication provided to business users regarding SLAs for Service Desk response times, categorisation of calls etc. A significant number of the business users demanded instant resolution of their Service Desk calls and queries. Senior management supported the business users' demands despite being made fully aware of the IT Services Supplier's achievement to contract and related SLAs. Senior management were not prepared to increase payments to the IT Services Supplier in improving the SLAs.

Relationships between the Head of IT and Contracts and supplier were amicable except during times of business critical system outages when the client became aggressive – due to senior management pressure – in demanding the supplier solve major incidents well within contractual SLAs. This problem was further compounded by a situation whereby the Head of IT had not ensured other supplier dependent contractual SLAs 'backed off' the main IT Service Supplier contractual SLAs – this created a situation whereby the IT Services Supplier was technically performing within their contractual SLA during major business critical outage incidents, overall, however, resolution of major incidents failed organisational SLA targets before they had even been logged.

At this point the client senior executives decided to appoint a new Head of IT. The new Head of IT lacked major programme, technical and contract management knowledge and experience; being more comfortable with having a supporting team of specialists reporting to him.

The new Head of IT inherited a 3 year business requirements driven fully layered – non product dependent - IT strategy which had been lead by a senior external consultant in consultation with key stakeholders and representatives from across the organisation. The strategy proposed a way forward which would lower IT support costs and fully exploit the existing technology in significantly enhancing the organisation's knowledge and information capabilities. Knowledge and information management were identified by the business as major areas of weakness; which created inefficient working practices. Additionally, the strategy allowed the organisation to keep its staffing levels static and provide to both internal business users and external customers a low cost, automated web-based self-service support and delivery mechanism.

The new Head of IT dismissed the IT strategy as it did not explicitly say which software/hardware solution to purchase (there was a separate IT Procurement Team with related processes and controls within the organisation) and set about 'in-sourcing' the IT function.

Twelve months on, the 3 year IT Strategy remained on the shelf, the organisation remained static in terms of its knowledge and information inefficiencies although the information problems had grown exponentially; business user satisfaction levels had further plummeted, costs of IT provision had spiralled and external stakeholder perceptions of the organisation had dipped due to the lack of interoperability regarding data and information transaction opportunities.

If things begin to go wrong

Sometimes, whatever you do and however skilled and prepared you are, your implementation project will begin to wobble.

Acept that this is quite normal! Remember you're a *change agent* and in only the most rare occasions will the whole organisation be behind you all the way.

The five main reasons that can usually cause an implementation project to go wrong include:

- Suppliers may provide you with unrealistic timescales or, discover inter-relationships and issues previously not identified. This may push your estimated timescales back and increase costs.

- Key project team members may leave the organisation; jeopardising achievement against plans.

- A radical change of senior management – with different priorities – may change the scope of the IT strategy or even stop the programme/project.

- The organisation's corporate strategy and/or business plans may radically alter, therefore, requiring a review of the strategy vision statements, aims and objectives.

- The IT strategy may be over ambitious and unachievable.

Should any of the above occur:

- Stay calm and try to alleviate any anxieties felt by the sponsor/director, sponsoring group, business group, technical forum etc.

- Persevere and get involved. This will provide you with a 'heads-up' of what's going on and why.

- Seek flexible ways in which you can adapt the IT strategy and implementation plans; use your communication skills and channels to reassure all affected.

 Keep smiling. "A smile is the light in the window of your face that tells people you're at home."

Highlights

✓ The personal qualities and characteristics of the implementation leader are as important as the IT strategy itself.

✓ Selecting an industry recognised programme or project management framework can increase your chances of success. See Appendix 1.

✓ Establish terms of reference (TOR) for your programme/project board, project sponsor/director, programme/project manager, business group and technical forum.

✓ Create timescaled programme or project plans – setting up workshops to help with planning expedites this activity.

✓ Assess and initiate risk management.

✓ Set up programme/project change management.

✓ Assess and initiate stakeholder management and communications.

✓ Proactively manage the programme/project, continually assessing progress and ensuring business alignment against the IT strategy's vision statement.

✓ Ensure you provide regular highlight reports to the programme/project sponsor/director and sponsoring group. Make sure these contain – as a minimum – programme/project progress against plans, the status of each work stream, issues and successes.

✓ If things go wrong, stay calm and be flexible in adapting to the changing circumstances and priorities.

Implementing the IT Strategy Checklist:

To assist you with implementing your IT strategy, complete the checklist below. For each question you answer with "no"; check to ensure you've given the question sufficient thought – that the activity or data and/or information regarding the question is not available to you, or is genuinely not relevant/required.

Question:	Yes	No
Has your organisation developed its own programme or project management framework?		
Do you think your implementation of the IT strategy is a programme or project?		
Do you already have a programme or project sponsor/director?		
Is it necessary to create a sponsoring group? (Does the culture expect it/need it?)		
Do you consider you have the personal qualities and characteristics essential to ensure the programme/project is a success?		
Are you confident of your ability to lead risk management activities?		
Are you confident of your ability to lead stakeholder management and communications activities?		
Does your organisation have a communications department/team?		
Does your organisation have a 'workshop' culture?		
Are you a confident facilitator of workshops?		
Do you have any training requirements?		
Are your training requirements going to be met in the short-term?		
If your organisation has a 'blame culture', do you plan to use an issues register and change management process to try to manage the programme/project more effectively?		

Chapter 4
Stage: Review

"We don't learn from doing.
We learn from thinking about what we've done."

The aim of this chapter is to assist you with ensuring a robust IT strategy review and governance process is in place, so that the IT strategy remains business aligned.

A highlight summary and checklist is included at the end of the section.

Reviewing the IT strategy

"How will we know when we've arrived?"

Given that an IT strategy is usually based on a three year time horizon, a lot of changes can occur prior to its full implementation, i.e. changes both inside the organisation and externally within the organisation's market sector.

Therefore, unless you regularly review your IT strategy against the corporate strategy or business plans, there's every possibility that you could come to the end of implementing it only to find it has not delivered what the organisation needed. Or, worse, discover that you've delivered what the organisation needed three years ago!

Setting up an IT steering committee can help to avoid such situations. It is sensible to initially populate your IT steering committee from members of the IT strategy business group, technical forum and programme/project sponsoring board. This will ensure your IT strategy is implemented and reaps the benefits initially identified.

If groups were not used to assist you in designing and developing your IT strategy then ideally the IT steering committee needs to comprise not only IT senior executives but also senior business representatives from around the organisation. Business representation will be particularly beneficial when implementing new or revised policies and procedures. The business representatives, by regularly participating in IT steering committee meetings and decision making, improve the up-take of new policies and procedures.

An IT strategy steering committee is most effective when it evolves from the IT strategy design and development groups.

The IT steering committee can provide the following benefits:

• Ensuring the IT strategy remains aligned to organisational strategy, aims and objectives throughout its implementation.

• Provides IT governance ('governance' concerns the rules, processes, procedures and behaviours that guide, monitor and affect the way the organisations powers are exercised).

• Provide prioritization for projects and programmes.

• Lead investment appraisals.

• Provide a 'guiding coalition' for any change initiatives, programmes and projects.

 A guiding coalition is a group of people all of whom have an interest (stake) in, and appreciation of the scope of, the IT strategy. They are a group of people who are in a position to validate the strategy, communicate achievements and make any necessary organisational, process and procedural changes.

Generic IT steering committee terms of reference are included to assist you in preparing your own. Ensure you gain the support of senior executives for the IT steering committee and associated terms of reference prior to inviting anyone!

IT Strategy Steering Committee

Proposed Terms of Reference:

To review and lead the development of the IT strategy including policies and priorities in line with business imperatives, leading IT investment appraisal exercises and facilitating open communications between business areas.

Proposed Objectives:
- Ensure the development and review of the IT strategy is aligned to the overall business strategy and operational needs.
- Governance and Review of IT policies.
- Provision of programme prioritisation.
- Act as an escalation point for programme issues and risks.
- Lead and review IT investment appraisal exercises; recommending how best to acquire appropriate funding for projects.
- Provide guidance and act as an enabling resource during any corporate reshaping or transformation initiative.
- Promote the use and purpose of the IT Steering Committee.

Funding Requirements:
Generally, funding for projects is approved by (name)

Membership:
Chair: CIO/Head of IT

Membership: A. N. Other (Director of (Department))
                A.N. Other (IT representation)
                A.N. Other (Business Representation)

Meeting Frequency:
The IT Steering Committee convenes every month as a minimum, or following the completion of any main IT strategy implementation stage/phase.

Highlights

✓ Setting up an IT steering committee maintains momentum for implementing the IT strategy – a guiding coalition – and ensures the strategy remains aligned to business needs and ambitions.

✓ IT steering committees are most effective when evolved from the IT strategy design, development and implementation business group, technical forum and programme/project sponsoring group.

✓ IT steering committees must have business representation for communications and buy-in purposes.

✓ If carefully drafted, an IT steering committee provides IT governance.

Reviewing the IT strategy checklist:

To assist you in ensuring the IT strategy is reviewed in a robust manner, complete the checklist below. For each question you answer with "no", check to ensure you've given the question sufficient thought – that the data and/or information regarding the question is not available to you or is genuinely not relevant/required.

Question:	Yes	No
Does your organisation already have an IT steering committee or similar?		
Does your organisational culture support proactive working groups such as IT steering committees?		
Have you/are you planning to implement your IT strategy by using a business group, technical forum and/or sponsoring group?		
Is the IT budget centralised?		
Do you think setting up an IT steering committee would improve your customers' perceptions of IT?		
Do you consider your key business stakeholders would welcome participation in an IT steering committee?		

Appendices

APPENDIX I

Industry Recognised Frameworks and Practices

TOGAF®

The Open Group Architecture Framework (TOGAF) was developed by members of The Open Group. The original development of TOGAF Version 1 in 1995 was based on the Technical Architecture Framework for Information Management (TAFIM), developed by the US Department of Defense (DoD)

TOGAF provides a comprehensive approach to the design, planning, implementation, and governance of enterprise architecture. The architecture is typically modelled at four levels or domains:

- Business
- Application
- Data
- Technology

A set of foundation architectures are provided to enable the architecture team to envision the current and future state of the architecture.

TOGAF provides a detailed, step-by-step method on how to build, maintain, and implement enterprise architecture. This method is the Architecture Development Method (ADM).

TOGAF benefits include:

- A more efficient IT operation.
- Better return on existing investment, reduced risk for future investment.
- Maximum return on investment in existing IT infrastructure.
- Faster, simpler and cheaper procurement.

- There is a clear strategy for future procurement and migration.

CoBIT®

Control Objects for Information and related Technology (CoBIT) is an open standard framework for IT management. It was created by the Information Systems Audit and Control Association (www.ISACA.org) and the IT Governance Institute (ITGI) in 1992 and is based on over 40 international standards.

COBIT provides a set of measures, indicators, processes and industry recommended practices to maximise the benefits of using IT. Additionally, COBIT provides an organisation with effective IT governance and control.

COBIT governance tools include:

- Management Guidelines
- A Process Framework
- Control Objectives
- Implementation Toolset
- Audit Guidelines

COBIT comprises 34 high-level processes with recommend control objectives, key performance indicators (KPIs), critical success factors and maturity models. The 34 high-level processes are clustered into four business domains:

- Planning and Organising
- Acquisition and Implementation
- Delivery and Support
- Monitoring and Evaluation

ITIL®

The IT Infrastructure Library (ITIL) is an industry recognised framework for managing the IT service lifecycle. The framework is owned and developed by the Office of Government Commerce (OGC).

The books are published by the UK Stationery Office (www.tsoshop.co.uk) and may be purchased direct from their Internet website.

MOF®

The Microsoft® Operational Framework (MOF) is owned and developed by Microsoft® Inc.

It is a framework very similar – and indeed aligned – to the ITIL® framework.

MSP®

First published in 1999, Managing Successful Programmes (MSP®) provides an industry recognised programme management framework. The core publication, "Managing Successful Programmes", is owned, developed and is the copyright of the UK Office of Government Commerce (OGC). The book is published by the UK Stationery Office (www.tsoshop.co.uk) and may be purchased direct from their Internet website.

Key components of MSP include:

* Managing the Change Process
* Programme Management Principles
* Programme Management Lifecycle

PMI®

PMI is a global professional association for project, programme and portfolio managers. Their main purpose is to advance the practice, science and profession of project management.

PMI offer their own certification, accreditations and project management training which include the following categories:

* Core Courses
* Specialist Courses
* Advanced Courses
* Business Analysis Courses

PRINCE2®

PRINCE2® provides a project management framework, concepts, processes and outline documentation including functional roles and document outlines. The core publication, "Managing Successful Projects with PRINCE2", is owned, developed and is the copyright of the UK Office of Government Commerce (OGC).

The book is published by the UK Stationery Office (www.tsoshop.co.uk) and may be purchased direct from their Internet website.

M_o_R®

The Management of Risk (M_o_R®) framework provides organisations with a flexible framework for assessing risk. The core publication is owned, developed and is the copyright of the UK Office of Government Commerce (OGC).

The book is published by the UK Stationery Office (www.tsoshop.co.uk) and may be purchased direct from their Internet website.

APPENDIX 2

Pareto Analysis

Vilfredo Pareto was an economist credited with establishing what is now widely known as the Pareto principle or '80/20 rule'.

When developing the principle he discovered that 80% of the land in Italy was owned by 20% of the population.

The Pareto principle may be used to help identify which systems or hardware are causing the most customer dissatisfaction or are creating the most recurring incidents/calls to the service desk.

Some sample 80/20 rule applications:

*   80% of process defects arise from 20% of the process issues.
*   20% of a sales force produces 80% of company revenues.
*   80% of customer complaints arise from 20% of products or services.

The Pareto effect even operates in quality management; 80% of problems usually stem from 20% of the causes.

Pareto charts are used to display the Pareto principle in action; arranging data so that the few vital factors that are causing the majority of the problems reveal themselves. Concentrating improvement efforts on these few will have a greater impact and be more cost effective than undirected efforts.

The main characteristics to look for in the Pareto chart are:

1.   A break point in the cumulative percentage line. This point occurs where the slope of the line begins to flatten out. The factors under the steepest part of the curve are the most important.

2.   Where there is no clear change in the slope of the line, look

for the factors that make up at least 60% of the problem. You can always improve these few, redo the Pareto analysis and discover the factors that have risen to the top now that the biggest ones have been improved.

3. If the bars are all similar sizes, or more than half of the categories are needed to make up the needed 60%, try a different breakdown of categories that might be more appropriate.

It is common for one Pareto chart to lead to another:

* Before and after charts.
* Charts that break down the most important factors discovered in an earlier chart.
* Charts that use different scales, such as number of complaints and the cost to respond, with the same categories.

Example:

Total calls	**450**		
Category	No. of Calls	%	Cumulative %
Bespoke 4	160	35.56	100
Bespoke 3	115	25.56	64
Bespoke 2	58	12.89	39
Email	43	9.56	26
Lotus Notes	32	7.11	16
User Error	15	3.33	9
Hardware	11	2.44	6
Printer	8	1.78	4
PowerPoint	6	1.33	2
Bespoke 1	2	0.44	0
Totals Check	**450**	100.00	

Set up the example using a spreadsheet application. The formula for the %

column, from the first line "Bespoke 4" is =sum(100/450)*160. For "Bespoke 3" the formula in the % column is =sum(100/450)*115. Calculate the remainder of the % column for each category item.

To calculate the Cumulative % column, the formula for row "Bespoke 1" is = sum(0+0.44). The formula for the row "PowerPoint 6" is = sum(0.44+1.33). Continue to calculate the cumulative % column working upwards.

[Note: Ensure your table of figures is not too long – no more than 10-12 rows/categories. Input the numbers and then calculate their percentages. When you have done this, sort your data 'high to low' – Data, Sort, Descending. You may now calculate the cumulative % column using the formula above.]

To create the chart below using Microsoft Excel, highlight the data table area and click Insert, Chart, Custom Types, Line – Column.

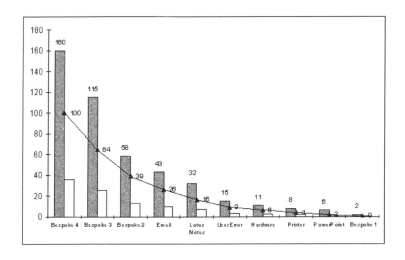

In the chart created above we can clearly see it is Bespoke 4 and Bespoke 3 that are causing the most errors.

APPENDIX 3

Return on Investment (ROI) Appraisal

Most organisations assess the feasibility of a project by calculating its estimated accounting rate of return (ARR) and, comparing it with a target ARR – usually set by management. The ARR is also known as 'return on investment' (ROI).

There are several methods of calculation for ROI. The most frequently used are:

$$\text{ROI} = \frac{\text{Estimated average profit}}{\text{Estimated average investment}} \times 100\%$$

$$\text{ROI} = \frac{\text{Estimated total profit}}{\text{Estimated initial investment}} \times 100\%$$

$$\text{ROI} = \frac{\text{Estimated average profit}}{\text{Estimated initial investment}} \times 100\%$$

In the above, 'profit' is the accounting profit based on accruals accounting principles and is normally taken after depreciation but before taxation. Taxation is ignored as it changes over time.

Example:

A business is considering a data centre server investment.

The target ROI for the business is 20%.

Initial investment for servers (cost of the assets): £80K.

Estimated life of servers: 4 years.

Estimated profit before depreciation:

Year	£ × 100
1	20
2	25
3	35
4	25

[Note: in the example, the servers are depreciated using the straight-line method; the servers have a nil residual value (in the company accounts) at the end of their 'life'. Therefore, the charge per year is £80,000/4 years = £20,000 per year.]

The annual profits after depreciation, and the mid year net book value of the asset for each year is:

Year	Profit after Depreciation (£ × 100)	Mid-year net book value (£ × 100)	ROI in the year %
1	0	70	0 (0/70000)*100
2	5	50	10 (5000/50000)*100
3	15	30	50 (15000/30000)*100
4	5	10	50 (5000/10000)*100

[Note: in the example, the mid-year book value is the value at the mid-point between the beginning of each year and the end of the year. For example, the value of the asset at the beginning of year 1 was £80,000 and at the end £60,000 (after deduction of depreciation of £20,000). The mid-year net book value is therefore £70,000.]

In the example, the investment does not achieve the target ROI of 20% in its first 2 years; however, it exceeds 20% in years 3 and 4 at a rate of 50%.

APPENDIX 4

Discounted Cash Flow

Because the ROI appraisal method (Appendix 3) does not take account of time and the value of money, the discounted cash flow (DCF) method is used by organisations as a more accurate investment appraisal technique. DCF is also commonly known as 'net present value' (NPV).

The discounting formula to calculate the present value of a future sum of money at the end of t time period is:

$$PV = FV * 1/(1+r)^t$$

PV is the initial or present value of the investment.

FV is the future value of the investment with interest.

r is the compound rate of return per time period.

t is the number of time periods.

Discounting may be applied to money receivable and to money payable at a future date. By discounting all payments and receipts from a capital investment to a present value, they may then be compared on a common basis at a value which takes account of *when* the various cash flows take place.

Example of using DCF in an Investment Appraisal

Company A is looking at a potential investment which it is anticipated will generate £40,000 after 2 years and another £30,000 after 3 years.

The target ROI is 12%.
The present value of these cash inflows is:

Year	Cash Flow ($£ \times 100$)	Discounted Factor 12%	Present Value $£$
2	40	$\dfrac{1}{(1.12)^2}$	31,888
3	30	$\dfrac{1}{(1.12)^3}$	21,353
		Total PV	**£53,241**

Note: In the example above "Year 3; Present Value £": the Microsoft Excel formula is =sum(30000*1/1.12^3).

Therefore, if company A can invest to earn a return of 12% on its investments now, it would have to invest £53,241 to earn £40,000 in 2 years time plus £30,000 in 3 years time.

Glossary

Architecture
Design, model.

Business Intelligence (BI)
A broad category of application programmes and technologies for gathering, storing, analysing, and providing access to data to help organisational users make better business decisions. BI applications include the activities of decision support, query and reporting, online analytical processing (OLAP), statistical analysis, forecasting, and data mining.

CEO
Chief Executive Officer

CIO
Chief Information Officer

Customer Intelligence
Tacit, explicit or unstructured explicit knowledge and information regarding what the organisation knows about its customers; whether in databases, survey responses, previous order history repositories, website statistics, customer feedback etc.

Customer Profiling
The process of using relevant and available information to describe the characteristics of a group of customers and to identify their discriminators from other customers or ordinary consumers and the drivers for their internet browsing, information retrieval, search activities or purchasing decisions.

Customer Relationship Management
A business philosophy involving identifying, understanding and better providing for your customers whilst building a relationship with each customer to improve customer satisfaction and maximise profits. It's about understanding, anticipating and responding to customers' needs.

Data Mining

Relates to the automated search and filter of large volumes of data with the aim of extracting new information and previously unrecognised relationships.

Data Warehousing

Involves retaining all data (or a copy of all data) at one location; this location is then remotely accessed from any location.

Distributed Systems Technologies

A non-centralised computer network; individual computers can communicate with one another and shared resources on servers. All resources appear to users as one area of storage, hardware etc.

Electronic Document Management System (EDMS)

An automated software system which provides creation and management controls for electronically created documents, emails etc.

Explicit Knowledge

Knowledge which is relatively easy to capture and store in databases and documents. It is shared with a high degree of accuracy. Explicit knowledge can be either structured or unstructured: Structured - Individual elements are organized in a particular way or schema for future retrieval. It includes documents, databases, and spreadsheets. Unstructured – the information contained is not referenced for retrieval. Examples include e-mail messages, images, training courses, and audio and video selections.

Information Architecture (IA)

IA is the term used to describe the structure of a system, i.e. the way information is grouped, the navigation methods and terminology used within the system. Effective IA enables people to step logically through a system confident they are getting closer to the information they require. Most people only notice IA when it is poor and stops them from finding the information they require. IA is most commonly associated with websites and intranets, but it can be used in the context of any information structures or computer systems.

Intellectual Capital

The sum of 'hidden' assets of a company. It comprises human resources, knowledge, intellectual property, knowledge of the customer and stakeholder relationships.

IT Governance

IT Governance is a term used to represent the system by which the current and future use of information technology (IT) is directed and controlled. It involves evaluating and directing the plans for the use of IT to support the organisation and monitoring this use to achieve plans. It includes the strategy and policies for using IT within an organisation. The primary goals for information technology governance are to (1) assure that the investments in IT generate business value, and (2) mitigate the risks that are associated with IT. This can be done by implementing an organisational structure with well-defined roles for the responsibility of information, business processes, applications, infrastructure, etc. IT Governance frequently uses established industry recognised frameworks and practices to achieve its goals, for example, ITIL, PRINCE2, TOGAF.

IT Infrastructure Library (ITIL)
IT Infrastructure Library. A set of best practice IT processes originally devised by the public sector (Office of Government Commerce) during the 1980's and now published by The Stationery Office. Version 2.0 was updated to ITIL version 3.0 in May 2007. An organisation's alignment to ITIL expedites auditing and certification against the international standard for IT Service Management; ISO:20000.

LAN
Local Area Network

Latent Needs
Customer needs the customer is not consciously aware of.

SAN
Storage Area Network

Sarbanes Oxley (SOX)
Following some highly publicised financial scandals in the USA, Congress enacted the Sarbanes-Oxley Act (2002). The act affects how public companies report financials and, significantly impacts IT. SOX requires more than documents and/or financial controls, it requires the assessment of a company's IT infrastructure, operations and personnel.

Stakeholder
Any person or group with a close interest, or stake, in the organisation and its success. For example, members, employees, board of directors, shareholders, unions, general public, customers, suppliers etc.

Systems Integration
Systems Integration is the process of linking applications in order to realise financial and operational competitive advantages. When different systems can't

share their data effectively, they create information bottlenecks that require human intervention in the form of decision making or data entry. With effective systems integration planning and architecture, organisations are able to focus most of their efforts on their value-creating core competencies instead of focusing on workflow management.

Tacit Knowledge

Knowledge people carry in their minds which is, therefore, difficult to access. People are often not aware of the knowledge they possess or how it can be valuable to others. Tacit knowledge is considered more valuable because it provides context for people, places, ideas, and experiences. Effective transfer of tacit knowledge generally requires extensive personal contact and/or trust.

Thin Client Technologies

A network computer without hard disk drives (a 'thin client') which accesses programs and data held on a server(s).

Further information & related organisations

Acerit Limited	**www.acerit.com**
American National Standards Institute (ANSI)	**www.ansi.org**
Australian Computer Society (ACS)	**www.acs.org.au**
British Computer Society (BCS)	**www.bcs.org**
Canadian Information Processing Society (CIPS)	**www.cips.ca**
European Union Computer Society (EUCS)	**www.eucs.org**
Internet Society	**www.isoc.org**
IT Service Management Forum (itSMF)	**www.itsmf.org**
International Standards Organisation (ISO)	**www.iso.org**
Information Architecture Institute	**www.iainstitute.org**
Information Systems Audit & Control Association (ISACA)	**www.isaca.org**
InterNIC	**www.internic.net**
Office of Government Commerce (United Kingdom)	**www.ogc.gov.uk**

Project Management Institute (PMI)	**www.pmi.org**
Software Engineering Institute, Carnegie Mellon University, Pittsburgh (SEI)	**www.cmu.edu**
The Institute of Risk Management (IRM)	**www.theirm.org**
The Open Group Architecture Forum (TOGAF)	**www.opengroup.org**
United States of America Government (USA)	**www.usa.gov**

NOTES

NOTES

Trademarks

CMM® /CMMI® are Registered Trade Marks of the Software Engineering Institute (SEI).

COBIT® is a Registered Trade Mark of ISACA/ITGI; Information Systems and Audit and Control Association / IT Governance Institute.

ITIL® is a Registered Trade Mark, and a Registered Community Trade Mark of the Office of Government Commerce, and is Registered in the U.S. Patent and Trademark Office.

MOF® is a Registered Trade Mark of Microsoft Corporation.

M_o_R® is a Registered Trade Mark and a Registered Community Trade Mark of the Office of Government Commerce.

MSP® is a Registered Trade Mark and a Registered Community Trade Mark of the Office of Government Commerce.

PRINCE® is a Registered Trade Mark and a Registered Community Trade Mark of the Office of Government Commerce, and is Registered in the U.S. Patent and Trademark Office.

PMI® is a Registered Trade Mark of the Project Management Institute. All rights reserved.

TOGAF® is a Registered Trade Mark of The Open Group.

The author acknowledges that there may be other company names and products that might be covered by trademark protection and advises the reader to verify them independently.